Praise for Dr. Adi Jaffe and the *IGNTD* Recovery Method

Starting Where You Are and Where You Want to Go

"A fresh and much needed perspective. Through his methodical research and personal life experience, Dr. Jaffe exposes some of the most dangerous myths in the recovery movement. This book is not only educational and eye opening, it is transformational for anyone struggling with addiction. Thank you Dr. Jaffe."

—Annie Grace, author of This Naked Mind

"Dr. Jaffe cuts through the mythology that engulfs addiction and presents us with scientifically backed ideas to help resolve this growing problem. This book is an absolute must-read for anyone who is struggling or trying to help someone and wants real solutions that are not based on hand-me-down wisdom."

—Andy Ramage, author of The 28 Day Alcohol-Free Challenge

" I cannot speak highly enough about the [IGNTD] work. I could probably write a book on just how much your methods have changed my life."

—IGNTD Recovery Online Course participant

"Dr. Jaffe, thank you for the most amazing experience that has changed my life forever, and for publicly sharing the story of your personal struggles... [It] gave me hope and confidence that I could change my behavior. I am excited for my future."

    —Workshop participant, Savannah, GA

"I feel so lucky to have found the IGNTD Recovery. It has been such an amazing mind shift to see that as my whole life improves my problems with substances also improve."

    —IGNTD Recovery Online Course participant

"Having Dr. Jaffe's help to get to the bottom of the problem and to dig deeper than just the substance abuse was tremendously helpful. Adi is a very positive person who helped transform my life in many ways besides helping with my substance abuse issues."

    —client, AM, Denver, CO

"What a relief to find IGNTD! I've tried other treatments for years but always hit a wall. If I questioned the program, I was told that I wasn't trying hard enough. It never felt like a good fit. It's great to be heard."

    —IGNTD Recovery Online Course participant

THE

A NEW APPROACH FOR

ABSTINENCE

OVERCOMING ADDICTION WITHOUT

MYTH

SHAME, JUDGMENT, OR RULES

ADI JAFFE, PHD

AN INTRODUCTION TO IGNTD RECOVERY

IGNTD Press

Visit IGNTD.com/Recovery for information about IGNTD
Recovery programs, workshops, and events, and to join the
IGNTD community.

To invite Dr. Jaffe to speak, please email speaking@igntd.com
For additional information or questions contact info@igntd.com

Published by IGNTD Press, Los Angeles, CA, USA
Editorial development by Janet Goldstein
First edition 2018

Print ISBN: 978-1-73223-940-1
eBook ISBN: 978-1-73223-941-8

To my parents, for being there when I needed them the most, my sister for putting up with the wreckage I'd caused for so long, and my wife and children for serving as the torch that lights up my days and nights.

"Hope is the foundational quality of all change."

—Alfred Adler, psychologist

CONTENTS

CHAPTER 1

WHAT I KNOW:

There Is Another Way

We all come from somewhere, with our own stories and histories. Though our stories don't determine who we become, they do shape our journey…

My Story

As early as elementary school, I began a fifteen-year journey to belong and find peace in my own skin. Of course, I didn't know it at the time. I thrived on the approval of teachers, peers, and my parents, and I was devastated when that approval wasn't there. Outwardly outgoing, a jokester, and a quick learner in school, inside I was filled with childish and then adolescent worries.

When alcohol came along as an option, everything changed. For me, there was a very specific catalyst. My general restlessness and the stress of dealing with the constant chatter in my brain had turned into social anxiety and shyness by the time I graduated from 'tween to teen. When I finally asked a girl out for the first time, the result was worse than anything I had imagined. The entire school found out that she turned me down, and I became a laughingstock. I was filled with shame and embarrassment.

1

Maybe someone else would have blown it off. But to me, the experience confirmed all the terrible thoughts I had about myself that I'd kept hidden. Now it was a fact: I would always be on the outside looking in, hanging out with the nobodies and being a nobody.

Two years later, my family had moved to the US and I found myself attending a teen leadership camp. On the last night, tucked away in one of the cabins, some boys started passing alcohol around. It was late, and there were so many kids in that cabin. I didn't want to embarrass myself again by sticking out, so I took a few swigs of the burning, clear liquid. Within minutes all my worries, nerves, and anxieties disappeared.

I still remember it like yesterday. There I was with the cool people, and I felt accepted. It was an epiphany that I could even feel this way. The grown-up activity I'd thought was "bad," "nasty," and "wrong" since childhood was instantly reframed in my mind as something good and positive. As awful as the taste was, it eased my mind. "I'll have more of that," became natural—"that" being the confidence and comfort that came with alcohol.

For years afterward, I outwardly tried hard to maintain my façade as a "cool," successful young person while my using, lying, acting out, and hiding only got worse. I drank, took all kinds of drugs, and got hooked on meth for five years. I went from using drugs to dealing them and living the fast life, essentially removed from reality. But the whole time I kept up a more "normal" facade—the myth that I was pursuing a career in music in LA, where I had transferred to finish college. I was good at lying and was given the benefit of the doubt way too many times, taking me farther and farther away from self-knowledge, acceptance, and any real connections. I was barely in touch with my family, constantly avoiding their calls after disappointing them endlessly. In spite of—or perhaps because of—all the drugs and using, I walked around with a constant stream of self-doubt and anxiety that would fill my head at any quiet moment . . . so I made sure to have as little quiet as possible. At twenty-five, I was going nowhere fast. Then I got arrested, and things got really bad.

Fortunately, after all this escalating use and drama, recovery programs and rebellion, rehab, jail (yes, I've been there), and tons of study and personal experimentation with recovery methods, I've been able to forge my way to a normal, healthy life that continues to unfold. Just saying "normal" means so much to me!

If you're reading this right now, "normal" probably sounds like the furthest thing from reality for yourself or someone very close to you. I've been clean of meth for fifteen years and drink moderately when socializing and celebrating. I work, have a family, have a life, and help others. I feel like I'm making a difference and my life matters. I belong.

The Current Recovery "System" Isn't Working

My journey to discover a way out of that personal hell began with my own recovery and tons of experimentation with the most traditional methods you can imagine as well as newer and alternative ones. I wanted answers for myself and for so many people I had met who were as hopeless as I'd once been or who didn't fit any descriptions I was familiar with. I knew there was something wrong with the "system" and the solutions it offered. Well, that's putting it kindly. The "system" demanded a solution—sometimes by force of law.

Drugs are killing more people than ever, and more users are being sent to jail than any other group. The only response we seem to keep coming up with is more of the same. While everyone argues about the true cause of addiction, the problem keeps getting worse. It's as though we're pushing harder on the gas pedal of a car as it's about to fly off a cliff. I wanted to turn the wheel.

My journey required a seven-year return to school, where I went on to study the psychology of addiction—how to measure it, the neuroscience behind it, and the data on what treatments worked and why. It was a long road, but one that was worth it. I now hold a PhD from UCLA, which offers one of the top psychology programs in the world. I've spoken to all kinds of groups, appeared on TV, written articles for popular publications, and even given TEDx talks. Throughout these experiences, I've seen firsthand how desperate people are for a new language and approach to recovery.

> *Addiction, the daily grind, the pressure and judgment we face, from both inside and out, wear us down and make us forget that it's possible to truly love our life.*

I've continued researching, teaching, and absorbing everything I could find about how to potentially change the current approach. I've worked directly with hundreds of individuals and families and have been fortunate enough to see recovery become real for them too. I began testing and applying my unique approach at the outpatient recovery center I co-founded and led for a number of years, and now in my own online programs, trainings, and individual support, I help make recovery possible for everyone— wherever they live and however they want recovery to fit into their lives.

I came to call my approach "The IGNTD Recovery Method" for a very specific reason. More than a recovery methodology, my goal is to ignite the greatness we all have within us.

Addiction, the daily grind, and the pressure and judgment we face both inside and out wear us down and make us forget that it's possible to truly love our life. The IGNTD Recovery Method teaches an approach to recovery—and life—that fits your brain, your body, and your world. It teaches you to choose inspiration over self-judgment and labels. It teaches that the goal is normal, rewarding, meaningful living, not a world of denial, abstinence, boredom, and loneliness.

I've worked with teens, young adults, businessmen and women, celebrities who seem to have it all, stay-at-home moms whose daytime drinking has led to drunk driving, and hardened drug addicts who still think deep inside they have a chance for a better life—and they do. I've helped family members and best friends rethink their "intervention" plans, finding that real love, honesty, and the embrace of someone who is struggling often goes a lot farther than 'tough love'. I've seen the change that's possible when we open up our minds and change our ideas of what addiction is and what recovery means. The way I see it, in the simplest terms:

"ADDICTION" OR "ABUSE" means that we, and our loved ones, experience our use as a problem (though no one is seeing the "real" problems underneath).

"RECOVERY" means that we, and our loved ones, experience our life getting better (and the "real" problems are getting addressed).

I've seen the huge transformations that take place when we widen our understanding of addiction and recovery and, in fact, have much bigger and more inspiring goals. When our hopes and aspirations are small and rigid, they actually work against us rather than serving as motivation for us. Here's what I know to be true:

- **Too much of what you've been told about addiction is wrong, misleading, and holding you back.** No matter who you are, no matter what your experience has been, I've learned that there's no need to be branded for life with the fear and burden that you will always be a loser, a drain on family and society, or one drink or pill away from devastation.

- **You are NOT your addiction, and hope is available to you right now.** You don't have to earn hope, and you certainly don't have to be perfect. Judgment, rules, false beliefs, and expectations make recovery a rare and special thing. But I know recovery can start with lessening the pain and taking very small steps.

- **There is more than one explanation for what addiction is and how to stop it.** Just as there are multiple definitions of what recovery means—definitions that are as unique as you are—there are multiple causes, vulnerabilities, circumstances, and personality types that lead to addiction, and there are multiple paths and tools that lead to recovery. Everyone has different dreams and aspirations as well as fears, traumas, and negative beliefs. The one-size-fits-all approaches only work for a small slice of people, and the evidence of this is all around us. For many others, the narrow pursuit of trying to fit everyone into one framework can actually do harm by missing important factors that are paramount to recovery.

- **Recovery doesn't require—or have to begin with—abstinence or the label of "addict."** We've defined "success" as abstinence—forever! And we define "failure" as anything else. This message is 100 percent wrong. We need to throw away the silly (and unsupported by research) notion that anyone who needs help must commit to lifelong abstinence from alcohol and drugs before they can begin their journey. (As we'll see, abstinence may be right for you, or right for you at certain times, but for others it is not.)

- **Thus, lifelong abstinence is the wrong goal (and is very rarely met).** This ill-formed goal hurts the potential for success of those who seek help and keeps lots more people from seeking any help at all. Right now, only 10 percent of people get help, and they often "fail" at what's offered. The vast majority aren't even on the "on ramp" to recovery. If we focus the help on what people actually want and what works for them, instead of on dogma and what we wish they'd do, we can substantially reduce the addiction problem starting today.

- **Recovery is not primarily about alcohol or drugs—it's not about use!** Drinking and using are NOT the problem—they are the cover-up of the problem(s). Just hold that thought for now. If all the focus is placed on drinking and using, that's the only thing you'll think about. The only thing you'll obsess about. The only thing that you'll think matters. But it's your life and the people in your life that matter. It's the experience you have inside your head and the feelings you're flooded with at every moment. It's your whole future, and what you'll do with it, that matters. That's what needs to improve.

- **Oh, and recovery doesn't have to be awful.** Yes, it takes work and effort, just as everything worthwhile does. But you can and will experience a better moment, a better day, a better week, a better conversation (even with yourself) while you make bigger changes and learn new approaches and tools to change your life. There will be moments of extreme pleasure and moments of pain. I call this the "deep-tissue massage" version of getting help. It's not always very relaxing, but it makes you feel a million times better after it's done. And as you continue using it, the pain lessens and the impact on your life is magnified.

So, those are a lot of "nots" about the IGNTD Recovery Method. But my system is actually more about saying yes. IGNTD Recovery is a way to uncover what anyone struggling with addiction is really after: a JUDGMENT-FREE, SHAME-FREE, RULES-FREE approach to saying YES TO LIFE! It's the only way this works.

The IGNTD Recovery Method— Starting Where *You* Are and Where *You* Want to Go

IGNTD Recovery isn't one-size-fits-all. It doesn't have paint-by-number steps. And I know that we can crave simple solutions—like alcohol and drugs—when we feel lost. But IGNTD Recovery is a progression of steps and a firm belief in YOU. I believe, and research shows us, that our minds are enormously powerful. As you learn and shift your understanding, you shift your ideas of what's possible, and what you're willing and excited to try.

> *One shift at a time, a new way of acting,*
> *being, and feeling becomes possible. You*
> *don't "do recovery"—you "do life."*

As you break free of your current ways of thinking, you become willing and excited to let go of old beliefs. One shift at a time, a new way of acting, being, and feeling becomes possible. You don't "do recovery"—you "do life."

My promises to you with this book are:

* **You'll learn to believe in yourself again.** Everyone, including you, can beat addiction. There are mountains of hope, and you can stop the struggle right now.

* **You'll stop being afraid and ashamed, and you'll start feeling excited and proud again.** You'll look tenderly at your shame, which has been festering for years, and you'll work through it. No judgments. No secrets. No comparisons. Just honesty and hope. The work will allow you to break free of your compulsive habits. But more, it will help you regain a deep sense of your own self-worth and ability.

* **You'll begin to see how you can move forward, and you'll start imagining the next chapter of your life.** Yes, you can regain the time, money, and relationships you've given away. The hardest first step is even imagining you can get your life back. You'll get the knowledge you need, along with my belief in you, to make that shift and imagine what's possible.

- **You'll get practical tools, stories, examples, and options to try so you can find *your* path to ignited recovery.** These are the tools you'll use for a lifetime of recovery measured by a full, meaningful, engaged life . . . a normal life. You'll use the ones that are relevant now and learn about others that may become useful in the future. Your tool kit will keep growing as your experience evolves.

- **You'll get so much more than a victory against your addictive behavior.** What surprised me most in my recovery were the benefits that went well beyond my drug use. I developed the most amazing relationships with everyone in my family. I learned how to communicate with others in an honest and intimate way. I am healthier, look better, feel better, and have greater financial success and stability. I pursued goals and hopes that I'd stopped daring to hope for. The blessings are nearly endless.

I want to give you a Get Out of Jail Free card—the jail that's been called "addiction." If you or a loved one is struggling with alcohol or drugs, there's a good chance you feel trapped and don't know if you can ever become free again.

EXERCISE: *Your Transformation Objective*

You're reading this book because you're looking for things to change. You may have found this introduction to IGNTD Recovery because you drink too much, smoke too much weed, watch too much porn, or engage in any number of other addictive behaviors.

But in order to be clear on how you are going to do this, it's important to know why you even want to. Because if you aren't clear about "why," you aren't going to do the work when it gets tough.

So here is a simple set of questions that will get you started on the path. No, they don't ask you how much you drink or how many grams of weed you smoke per week. The focus for now is much simpler—and much more profound:

1. What is the biggest change IGNTD Recovery could help you create if it worked?

2. If you could achieve that transformation, what change would it deliver in your life?

3. In what incredible ways would success transform your current reality?

CHAPTER 2

THE MYTHOLOGY OF ADDICTION

A Misguided Goal Leads to a Misguided Path

People love it when I tell my story. I've told it on stages in front of thousands of people—to students, parents, conference attendees, counselors and psychologists, addiction experts, and so many more. I found out a few years after I started speaking in public that there's a name for it. It's called "The Hero's Journey."

I definitely didn't feel like a hero, given the mess I'd created for so many people in my life. My story felt much more complicated and involved than that. But no matter how much of my struggle I shared, most people didn't see me as a loser or criminal or a recovered addict. "Hero" is what they take away. At least that's what they tell me.

It took me a while to realize why people responded to my story the way they did, especially because I'd been told so many times that I shouldn't tell it. Mentors counseled me to keep my history of addiction a secret—for my own recovery and because the information would taint everything else I wanted to do. They thought it would pigeonhole me as someone with a cause rather than a good scientist or professor.

But the way I saw it, it was a good thing to have a cause. It gave me purpose. It gave me a reason to keep doing all the hard work that lay ahead. When I was just starting out in my professional life—and years away from getting my PhD, it was the only thing that actually kept me motivated and hopeful. So I didn't listen to the advice, and gradually I started telling the story of my hero's journey more and more publicly.

Not everyone likes my story. Not everyone likes the approach I took and how I define—and sometimes defy—the path of recovery. But putting the topic of "methods" aside, my message fits most people's model of a hero. I look the part of a "success story" (I dress nicely for many of these talks and presentations). I sound right (my foreign accent is pretty spot-on at this point in my life, with just a hint of my Israeli coming through). Plus, I have the letters "PhD" after my name, which makes my hero's journey "official." It all fits perfectly—from the outside.

Even though I talk often about the devastating setbacks I faced and the fear that still rears its head when my anxieties get the best of me, people grab on to the heroic aspect of my story and the belief that it signals that a better life is possible.

> *The characters we play in our lives become more real and more known than the full human beings we are.*

Since the earliest days of storytelling and folk tales, myths and fairy tales, we've loved stories that fit the templates embedded in our psyches. We love having familiar heroes and villains in our books, movies, and plays—even when the play is real life. We love the comeback kid and the heroic story of triumph over adversity. I see it with the people I work with all the time. The characters we play in our lives become more real and more known than the full human beings we are.

"From Party Girl to Lost Mom… to a Way Out" (Terry's Story)

When I started working with people struggling with addiction issues, I found out that "closet drinking" was actually a real thing. People who become so desperate to avoid their shame and hide their drinking from their loved ones can actually find themselves "sneaking" alcohol in closets and pantries.

It seems far-fetched, but I've heard dozens and dozens of similar stories. They all tell the tale of a person deeply entrenched in a compulsive and unshakeable use of alcohol or drugs, no matter the mounting consequences and pressure to stop.

Terry's Spiral Downward

Terry came to see me with such a story. She had been drinking too much for about ten years. Married with two children, she seemingly had the perfect life: a beautiful house in sunny Orange County, California, with beautiful children who swam in the beautiful pool in the backyard.

Starting in college, Terry had always been a pretty heavy drinker—but wasn't that par for the course? She had a reputation as a party girl and knew how to have a good time. In her twenties she kept up her carefree ways after work hours, but more recently, as a married, stressed-out, forty-five-year-old mother of two, the intensity of her drinking had taken a turn and reached levels she'd never imagined were possible.

Terry would regularly start drinking at lunch—maybe a glass of wine or champagne with friends. She would continue back at home, refilling her glass before her kids returned from school. Usually she picked them up, so she kept her drinking to a minimum (though omnipresent) because she didn't want her driving to be compromised, but once the kids were home, Terry's drinking would escalate. She would have a few glasses of wine before dinner and a few more while everyone was seated at the table. By the end of the night, Terry would end up drinking at least at least one bottle of wine, but usually two, per night. When her husband began notic-ing, she slowed down at the dinner table, but would sneak an extra drink or two in the kitchen as she brought out the food. It was becoming obvious, though, as nearly every night would end with her passing out, drunk.

Her husband was on to her, so her sneaking became more extreme. Eventually she found herself hiding a bottle of vodka in her tall black boots in her beautiful walk-in closet. She'd take a few gulps (God, how it burned initially!) of the warm vodka before dinner. Typically she found herself having a few more swigs after dinner, as she got ready for bed.

Terry never thought she would end up an "alcoholic." But after an accumulation of lost nights, too many fights to remember, all the mornings swearing she would slow down and stop, and all the failed attempts, she now knew she was an alcoholic. There was no other explanation.

Recently her husband's resentment toward her constant drinking had reached a fever pitch. He had "put his foot down," according to Terry, after a night when they'd actually had friends over to the house for dinner like old times. As the tension rose around her ducking into the kitchen to drink more than was "acceptable," all hell broke loose between them and was on display for all to see. Terry was really drunk and said some things she wished she hadn't—at least not so loudly and in front of their friends.

After that horrible night, Terry tried hard to cut down but she wasn't able to stop. She went to some AA meetings, but she *hated* the public humil-iation of sharing her experiences, and she wasn't sure she could stop drink-ing forever. She certainly knew she didn't want to. She hated the notion of never being able to have a cocktail with friends or a toast at a wedding.

All Terry could see ahead of her was a life as an alcoholic—or a recov-ering one if she could ever manage it. It felt like an embarrassing tragedy, not the fairy tale she imagined when she first got married.

All Terry could see ahead of her was a life as an alcoholic—or a recovering one if she could ever manage it. It felt like an embarrassing tragedy, not the fairy tale she imagined when she first got married.

Terry's Way Back Out—Looking for WHY, Not WHAT

Terry heard from a friend that I had a different way of helping alcoholics. In desperation she made an appointment to see me. Her tears began the moment she sat down. Crying, she told me she was ready to do (almost) anything for her nightmare to stop. She never imagined her life being tormented by the alcohol that used to be so much fun for her.

The trouble with so many stories like Terry's is that by the time someone comes to see me, a whole mountain of negative consequences have amassed. No one comes in for help at the very start. By the time they sit in front of me, the client, their family, and anyone else involved has been focusing on the drinking for so long that it's the only thing they can seem to pay attention to. And they want it to stop *now!*

Terry was focused on that too. She expected me to ask questions about her drinking—how much, what kind, for how long, and so on. And I did. But then I asked her a different kind of question, one she wasn't expecting.

After a short pause, I took a deep breath and asked Terry when she first noticed that her drinking was a problem.

Terry began by explaining that she noticed everything changing and her drinking getting worse after her kids were born. She basically described herself as the stereotype in her mind. She saw herself as the stay-at-home mother who drank to cope with her overwhelm and boredom- and as a way to bond with the other moms in her circle.

I paused again. Terry understood *what* was wrong- her drinking- and didn't need convincing there. But I wanted her to see *why* she was drinking and what the drinking might be covering up. While her explanation uncovered the character she'd become in her life, I wanted to see what was underneath. To help Terry, I wanted to understand:

- Why was she drinking more than usual?
- Why did she keep feeling that having more wine seemed like a good idea?
- Why was she having a problem reducing the amount she drank?
- Why was it easier for Terry to hide her drinking than be honest about it?
- Why did she want to numb herself regularly?

In order to begin digging deeper, I asked Terry to visualize her life over the past twelve months and describe what had been going on and how she'd been feeling.

Terry initially was at a loss for words. It was as though her life had a big hole in it. Aside from her embarrassment and shame around her drinking and her anger about her failures, she wasn't aware of feeling much at all.

Terry told me about dinners at home when her husband would remove the bottle of wine, leading to fights and a period lasting several months when he was determined to eliminate all the alcohol in the house—only he resented this because it meant he couldn't drink at home either, which caused more fights.

Terry believed that her husband meant well, but all his focus was on her drinking. Nothing else seemed to matter, even when she made the effort to get the house in order or plan a weekend away where she was sure she wouldn't make a fool of herself. Her husband seemed oblivious to everything but the drinking and how it was ruining his life and focus at work. He didn't even pay much attention to the kids anymore. Though Terry didn't say it then, I could hear the loneliness in her voice.

I explained to Terry that her husband was typical, not exceptional. In the beginning, well before the problem had reached epic proportions, moments almost always present themselves when it makes sense to examine "why" the drinking is going on. But it rarely happens. And when it does, it's often cursory—with everyone giving the benefit of the doubt. For the most part, everyone fixates on the visible behavior rather than the feelings or circumstances driving it.

For the most part, everyone fixates on the visible behavior rather than the feelings or circumstances driving it.

Later on, when the alcohol (or drug) use is extreme and incomprehensible, it's easy to understand why it's difficult to focus on anything else. But when the problem is new, simple attentiveness and concern can make all the difference and shift the progression, which for most people is not inevitable. Just imagine, for a moment, Terry's husband saying:

"Hey love, I see you drinking way more than usual. . . . Are you okay? What's going on? Can I help?"

But that attentiveness means peeking around the corner and looking at what's really going on—without panic, anger, judgment, or resentment overtaking the situation. Unfortunately, many times people aren't paying attention, don't want to know what's going on, or have no idea how to address it.

That was the end of our first session. Terry broke the spell of alcohol as the only important thing in her life, and we talked about why it's important to dig deep below the surface of the crisis and look around the corner.

I asked Terry if she wanted to continue working together, suggesting that she commit to appointments for the next month; that way it wouldn't be too scary or too extreme, like traditional programs. I explained that we'd look at what was going on, and she would make decisions about when and if she wanted to change her drinking. Our sessions would give her a safe place to think and observe her life, and I'd give her strategies to cope in the short term while we developed long-term plans.

During the next few sessions, Terry talked more and more about her marriage and began "unpacking" her relationship.

It turned out that Terry and her husband had been on the outs for a long time. Their relationship suffered early on when he became progressively more devoted to his work and less focused on them as a couple. She was expected to figure everything out with the kids—all the decisions, logistics, and worry. She hadn't realized how stressful that was for her.

Terry struggled to cope, but she believed it was absolutely the only way forward for her. The other moms were in the same situation, and they didn't seem to have as hard a time, although most of them had more hired help than she did. Terry would complain to her husband on occasion, but mostly she would drink and commiserate with her friends because she felt that they understood her. Plus, her social life always had made her happy, and she wanted to fit in and keep up.

Terry was playing a role she was committed to playing, no matter how hard the role had become. But then she just couldn't do it anymore.

By the time Terry's drinking had escalated, she and her husband were no longer just distant, they had completely lost any measure of intimacy between them, with sex being a distant memory. They barely talked about anything other than logistics, and they fought all the time. Terry felt trapped.

Terry was playing a role she was committed to playing, no matter how hard the role had become. But then she just couldn't do it anymore.

The only thing Terry relished were the hours she spent with her sister, who also was a heavy drinker, or her friends who started with drinks at lunchtime at one of their houses or at some pretty restaurant in the neighborhood. She loved those long conversations and the connection she felt she had with those women—the connection she missed so much at home. They'd complain about their individual troubles and commiserate with each other. So she went to more lunches, invited her sister over to the house more, and gradually became more accustomed to daytime drinking that lasted into the night.

It turned out she hadn't felt as if she "belonged" with her husband for a long time. The fun times that sparked their connection when they met had turned into a battle of wills—she was the bad one, the unreliable one, the weak one. He was the provider, the success story, and the rule maker. She hated who she'd become—not just the drinking, but what she was doing with her whole life.

We'd gone past our first month, and it was already becoming apparent that addressing Terry's relationship with her husband would require serious effort. Terry had slowed her drinking, started taking long walks in the park near her kids' school and, with the tiniest bit of optimism, began looking for a local couples therapist who could potentially help them restore what they originally had. Unfortunately, her husband wasn't all that interested in working on the relationship. He believed that everything would be fine if only Terry could manage to stop her drinking.

Disappointed, Terry found herself feeling alone once again. But with the support of our sessions and what she was learning, Terry continued working on herself. She was no longer so afraid of what thoughts might come into her head. She understood that the WHY of her drinking was as important as the drinking itself, even if it was hard to accept, and even if she didn't yet know what to do about any of it or how everything would turn out.

Terry's Present Reality—It's About Life

About three months into our work together, a radical new series of ideas emerged for Terry:

- What if she could have a life she actually wanted?

- What if she didn't have to simply accept living miserably?

- What if reducing her drinking would get her there?

Up to that point, Terry would go back and forth between days of abstinence, days of drinking a couple of glasses of wine, and days of drinking until she passed out. Overall her use was way down, and yet she still felt like a failure for not meeting everyone's expectations. But suddenly it was like a switch went on in her mind: Drinking less no longer seemed like an awful challenge, but like a challenging opportunity!

The road for Terry was longer and more far-reaching than she could ever have imagined. While she came to me seeking help with alcohol, she quickly realized she wanted help with her life. With the focus taken off her drinking and our sessions focused on her marriage and goals, her use of alcohol slowed down, and she felt like she was looking at her life for the first time in years. She and her husband separated, which she never could have imagined before, but she felt a sense of freedom for the first time in years.

While Terry came to me seeking help with alcohol, she realized she wanted help with her life.

Terry and her husband planned to try and work things out, but for the immediate future, Terry needed to feel like she was back in control of her life. With her husband gone from the house, so was the most consistent reminder that her life had taken a wrong turn along the way—and Terry began taking a more proactive approach to every element of her life. Little by little, it was as if the ordinary "scenes" that made up her day began to change. Click. Click. Click. The scrapbook of her life was evolving. For example:

* Terry had joined a gym long ago and had been exercising regularly, but now she began paying attention to her inner well-being, not just her weight and looks. She started taking Yoga classes, and that led her to start meditating for a few minutes every day.

* She started thinking about downtime as a chance to reflect, and she made sure to take time to journal about how she felt every day.

* She was discovering what she liked to do in life and working hard to remove the notion that she was somehow trapped due to circumstances.

* As she found her footing, Terry discovered that alcohol played a less and less important part in her life. Nevertheless, she was still relying on it too much to cope with her loneliness and stress at the end of the day.

* She changed her routines so lunchtime was spent at the gym, walking, or engaging in some other activity that fulfilled her, and she distanced herself from the friends who spent their afternoons drinking.

* She introduced biofeedback work to improve her ability to relax and help her sleep better.

* In addition to all these changes, Terry decided to take an extended break from drinking. She wanted to learn how to take care of

herself. She made her own decision, one she couldn't imagine before, to remove drinking from her life.

The Wider Lesson—Getting to the Tender, Hidden Spots

An unhappy relationship is a common problem. One partner typically feels as if they are unheard, unappreciated, or otherwise mistreated. However, alcohol can become a substitute for speaking up and taking care of the issue. It can "take the edge off," when the true purpose of the edge is to remind us that we need to develop better communication and healthier intimacy.

Early on no one seems to notice or particularly care. The alcohol *helps* tensions subside, and things may seem to fall back in line. But unless someone starts paying attention to the underlying issues, the relationship continues deteriorating because no work is being done to fix it. And the drinking has to keep up. Inevitably, by the time the partner wakes up and pays glaring attention, it's obvious what's wrong: the drinking has gotten out of hand. The solution is therefore clear as well: the drinking must stop.

Now the real struggle begins. Two people who may have been resentful of one another for years—and missed or glossed over so many signals—put all the focus on trying to fix the problem right in front of them, which is resolving the "alcoholic's" drinking problem. The fact that the marriage has been falling apart for far longer is nowhere on the agenda, and neither is a real long-term solution.

The better approach, in many of these situations, begins with stabilizing the alcohol use—without the label and focus on "recovery" and "abstinence"—and starting the "deep tissue massage" of awareness and change.

The better approach, in many of these
situations, begins with stabilizing the
alcohol use—without the label and focus on
"recovery" and "abstinence"—and starting
the "deep tissue massage" of awareness
and change.

Inevitably, a therapist, counselor, or coach ends up reaching the points of discomfort, the knots—or buttons—that make the couple respond. While certainly loaded with emotion, that's where much of the needed work hides. If both partners are willing and able to put in the effort, real magic can happen, which I've seen in my own life. If the work is only taken on by one person in a couple, or one person in a family, transformation still happens, but since families operate as little social systems, this sort of change in one part of the whole can lead to separate paths- and a healthier and happier one for the 'addict'.

EXERCISE: Starting Your Journey

Terry came to me to deal with her drinking, but she found out there were a lot of other issues below the surface. She discovered aspects of her life that had created difficulties for years, difficulties that she'd hidden from herself and ignored.

Those discoveries led Terry to make some decisions that surprised even her and ultimately led to her journey toward a fulfilling life. It was a journey to have a life devoid of alcohol problems *and* a way of living devoid of the avoidance she had become so used to.

Now it's your turn. Why are you here? What's your journey with addiction? What might be your journey with the issues you've avoided?

1. What is the primary addiction problem you are seeking help with?

2. If you step back and take a look at your overall life, what other areas have been a struggle for a while? (Think of your education, career, intimacy, health, life purpose, family, adventure, creativity, joy.)

3. What precipitating events have occurred in your life in the last twelve months that have you made you:

    a. Become more engrossed in your addictive behavior?

    b. Make a decision to address your addiction?

CHAPTER 3

THE POWER OF STORIES

Getting Stuck in a Role

We create stories and rationales for the way we see things in order to make sense of the world around us. This is the origin of mythology—the collected stories people tell to explain nature, history, and customs even when new knowledge eventually may prove we were completely wrong. It's the story of Zeus, the Greek god of thunder and lightning, of Prometheus as humanity's source of fire, and of gullible Eve and the snake as the origin of sin—old stories whose original purpose we've outgrown.

The trouble with Terry's story is that, just like me, she checked off too many boxes for a character she was very good at playing. She was the well-off suburban mom. All the other signals were ignored until it was almost too late.

Like the stereotype, Terry was pretty, had beautiful clothes, beautiful children, and the time and money to spend with friends at leisurely lunches. But Terry's role had started to fall apart long ago, before she'd even noticed.

When we have a character to play, we do our damnedest to play it well. Everyone sees us as that character, in part because we do such a good job of playing our role and in part because it's easy for others to suspend their disbelief and overlook the telltale signs that it's all a sham.

The Pygmalion Effect

There's a name for this constant and reciprocal relationship between individuals and those around them. It's called the "Pygmalion effect," after the Greek myth in which the character of Pygmalion, who had sworn off women, sculpted his own version of the perfect woman in marble. Pygmalion was so in love with his statue that he started treating his creation like a real woman, feeding and bathing her as if she were alive. The gods, seeing Pygmalion's love for his creation, decided to grant him his true wish, turning the statue into a real, live woman.

The Pygmalion effect, notably studied by psychologist Robert Rosenthal, shows us that what we believe about others actually affects their behavior in subtle and not so subtle ways. For instance, in one study Rosenthal showed that simply leading elementary school teachers to *believe* that some of their students were "intellectual bloomers" actually increased the IQ scores of those students over the academic year.

The Pygmalion effect is powerful in its own right, making us "act" a part based on the beliefs and expectations of others. When paired with another well-studied psychological phenomenon called "confirmation basis," its power is amplified even further.

> *The Pygmalion effect is powerful in its own right, making us "act" a part based on the beliefs and expectations of others.*

How Confirmation Bias Tricks Us

For decades we've known that our brains organize information into the expected and the unexpected. Once a belief is established, our brains selectively pay attention to information that falls in line with our beliefs rather than information that contradicts- or expands- them. Confirmation bias is a simple and efficient mechanism to organize information as important or not. However, it also encourages us to pay less attention to details by allowing us to make assumptions that fall in line with our existing beliefs and experiences. In a classroom setting, confirmation bias encourages teachers to see the "good girl" as always helpful and nice and overlook the times she may be the troublemaker or instigator. In politics, confirmation bias is a big part of the reason for our ongoing and intransient divisions.

> *Once a belief is established, our brains selectively pay attention to information that falls in line with our beliefs rather than information that contradicts—or expands—it.*

If we come back to a suburban mom like Terry, confirmation bias held for her husband and friends until the point she was sneaking alcohol and passing out drunk at night. Although even then, it took that drunken disaster of a party to truly make everyone pay attention.

When it comes to drugs and alcohol, we've created some specific myths and characters. We can think of these as modern archetypes. They allow us to categorize and explain behavior without paying attention to the finer details of what's really going on beneath the surface. For example:

- The high-powered, play hard/work hard executive who drinks through meetings over lunch and dinner, closes deals, and takes no prisoners.

- The stay-at-home mom who may be lonely, depressed, bored, or overwhelmed.

- The life of the party—man or woman—who knows how to have fun and is the unabashed pied piper for all revelers.

- The rebel or explorer, the risk-taker who uses substances as a way to belong to a counterculture and escape the straight-and-narrow, "boring" status quo.

- The social lubricator who uses substances to ease conversation, fit in with different groups, and make socializing easier both for themselves and everyone around them. (Maybe they're the people who sing karaoke with their friends at the bar?)

- The neurotic one who, without the calming effect of drugs, becomes the edgy friend who sees and feels everything a bit more intensely than everyone else, but with a depth that is admired and perhaps seen as appealingly mysterious.

- The introvert (or loner, depending on your point of view) who likes to hang out alone, with drinking as a solo activity to help reflect and pass the time.

Many of us fit into more than one archetype. I was the rebel and a social lubricator—I couldn't have been one without the other. Terry was the stay-at-home mom with a lingering reputation as the life of the party that she still carried from her high school and college days.

We take on these roles to play our part in the "story" of our families and relationships. We hold on to these roles ever tighter until the Mythology of Addiction rears its head, and "addict" becomes the only identity we have. Once you find yourself labeled an "addict"—by yourself or the people around you—you're no longer the rebel, mom, executive, social lubricator, or anxious neurotic one. You've crossed over. Once the drinking (or drug use) gets so extreme and public that there's no denying it, the only explanation is "addiction." And the only "cure" is abstinence—nothing else matters.

The collective Mythology of Addiction has taught us all: once an addict, always an addict. It's now clear what the growing problems have been about. You have a problem. You have a problem because you're an alcoholic. You have a disease.

Of course, an executive who manages to drink all day while working but comes home and can't take care of his responsibilities and relationships because he gets drunk on the weekends does, indeed, have a problem. But that problem only scratches the surface. There are likely a number of others—communication and intimacy issues with his wife, problems he's been having at work, shame about people always covering up for him (which he tries hard never to think about). He may also have been saddled with a biological predisposition toward anxiety and an early childhood trauma he's told no one about. But as long as we simply say, "Oh, he's an alcoholic," none of these things seem to matter.

The confirmation bias means that the addiction is all we see. Only if we pay close attention do we also see the fact that he's also a great friend; his clients love him, even if he's sometimes a bit outrageous and not great with the spreadsheet details; and he's really smart and his insights really make you stop and think.

Terry was a beautiful, spunky, happy person—she wasn't a sad or hard-to-manage child or teenager. She wasn't the most ambitious person, but she always had friends and did well enough. Yet once her drinking moved from a social function to a survival one as a wife and mother and her unhappiness grew, she became "an alcoholic." It was the way she saw herself now, and certainly the way her husband saw her. Eventually that became the only thing people could see. It confirmed in their minds that she drank too much because she was an alcoholic; thus she had to stop drinking. Nothing else much mattered.

For many people, abstinence *is* the best solution, but no matter what, being addicted doesn't mean that nothing else in life matters. In fact, as we'll see in Chapter 4, when we take some of the spotlight off the addiction, it widens the stage of what's going on and makes recovery, drinking less, and abstinence much more possible.

> *For many people, abstinence is the best solution, but no matter what, being addicted doesn't mean that nothing else in life matters.*

Widening Our Lens

The way we look at the problem keeps everyone trapped. In Terry's case, the focus stayed on Terry, and her husband believed that if she got fixed, everything would be okay. For a little while that worked. They'd have a big fight, Terry would cut back and wouldn't drink in public, and they'd calm down and spend some time together as a couple. But then the same old things that were wrong before continued being wrong and eventually pushed Terry back to drinking heavily. Everyone thought she "relapsed" because she was an alcoholic, and alcoholics can't control their drinking. Thus the cycle repeats over and over and over. Terry tried different approaches— her husband didn't, though, because *he's* not the alcoholic, and alcohol is the problem. But even though everyone told Terry that when she stopped drinking, everything will get better, it didn't. And that made Terry and her husband and their friends feel hopeless.

Everyone had been saying that as soon as the drinking stops, everything will get better. But it didn't.

Imagine how things could change if we got past our confirmation bias and the wish-fulfilling prophecy of the Pygmalion effect.

* What if Terry had let people see her imperfections and they accepted them?

* What if Terry saw her role not as someone who needed to handle everything and smile through it but as someone who deserved to ask for help when she needed it?

* What if we saw Terry as a woman who was out of sorts, not because her drinking was out of control but because she needed to rely on drinking to be able to handle her life?

* What if Terry's friends asked her if they could help?

* What if Terry's husband wondered why she was drinking more than usual around the dinner table or supported her in getting child care and help around the house?

What might have changed? Would Terry's husband cut down on his travel to be at home more with his wife? Together would they have decided to get help for their relationship?

The answers aren't clear, because it's difficult to predict what would have happened if circumstances were different. But we know that when these types of issues are addressed, recovery from alcohol and drugs is substantially more likely to happen. Even more importantly, as far as I'm concerned, the people who have this sort of experience in recovery—deep help that addresses all of the underlying issues and NOT just the drinking—end up actually enjoying, rather than resenting, their recovery.

People who have the experience in recovery of addressing the underlying issues and stories—and NOT just the drinking—actually end up enjoying, rather than resenting, their recovery.

Of course, many good treatment centers address additional issues on top of the elimination of drinking, but so many people who need help won't start the conversation when the only solution that's put in front of them is complete abstinence. Yet the industry persists.

That's why only 10 percent of people who need help with addiction issues get help. It's not because they don't know they have a problem (the denial explanation), it's not because they're liars, and it's not because they can't make rational decisions. It's because we've somehow decided that, unless they are willing to accept this first rule—complete abstinence—they are not prepared for help.

But it isn't true. It's never been true, and it's one of the primary reasons for too many deaths, too many lives destroyed, and too much collateral damage in the form of incarceration, broken homes, and shattered childhoods.

What would happen if we saw through the Abstinence Myth as the end-all-be-all cure for addiction? What if we had a new, truer, broader, and more complex understanding of the real meaning and causes of addiction? What if we could, as we've managed to do with classic mythology, finally accept that the world isn't flat and addiction isn't one thing for all people?

What if we could bury the Abstinence Myth and see it instead as one path for recovery from addiction, but not *the* path for all those who struggle with addiction, and especially not for all the myriad issues of life that make addiction possible and help it take hold of our lives?

EXERCISE: *Identifying the Roles You Play*

In Terry's story, the roles of "stay-at-home mom" and "party girl" seemed to fit and explain her sense of self and the way others saw her—until the cracks were too obvious to hide.

Sometimes finding "stories" or "archetypes" we fit into can give us shortcuts to our true experience in the world. They can also keep us stuck in roles where we stop growing and changing. They can enable us to avoid uncomfortable truths, the pain that comes with them, and the growth that dealing with them might offer.

Think about the roles and archetypes that may be helping you and holding you back:

1. Identify your leading archetypes. What role do you see yourself playing in the world? (For example, are you a combination of play hard/work hard executive; stay-at-home mom; good-time party person; rebel or explorer; social lubricator; troubled or neurotic one; introvert or loner; or other roles?)

2. Write down the characteristics you believe define the roles you identified. Think in terms of the archetypal characteristics, whether or not you feel they apply to you.

3. Circle the characteristics you listed above that you believe actually fit your life and your personality. Put a line through those that are not representative of you. You will likely find that a good portion of your adopted "role" does not fit with the way you see yourself.

4. What are one or two beliefs included in that list that may have held you back?

5. What are one or two strengths you possess that you have been ignoring because they didn't fit your archetype?

6. What relationships in your life (including those related to your addictive behavior) are being affected by these unrealistic expectations?

CHAPTER 4

THE POWER OF EXPLANATIONS

Getting Stuck in What We Already Know

You've heard it said many times. Maybe you've said it yourself:

Aren't all addicts basically the same—don't they have an uncontrollable problem with alcohol or drugs, and the only solution is to stop using?

I hate this question—along with the answer it assumes. Do you know why?

It's not because it's dismissive and disregards the individual experiences of the people I work with (although it does). It's not because it ignores what many of us know deep inside (although it does). It's because it is one of those questions that is asked rhetorically, as if the only true answer is a resounding yes.

But that's crazy. I've researched, met, and worked with all kinds of people with alcohol problems ("alcoholics") and those who use drugs ("drug addicts"). And I've come to one deceptively simple conclusion: Everyone is unique, and everyone shares common characteristics.

The deep sense of shame, embarrassment, guilt, and hopelessness is universal.

But just as important are the differences—our personal histories, environmental influences, biology, and levels of resiliency are all individual. Moreover, the ways these factors combine and contribute to addiction are nearly endless.

Only you have the power to understand yourself and where you want to go. Only you know if you really have what it takes to beat addiction down. Only you know if, like Terry, you're sick and tired enough to do all the work that's necessary to recover and make your life better.

Only you know whether you're going to quit your recovery journey when it gets tough *and* whether a small—or major—relapse will make you slip back into oblivion or come back twice as strong because you finally figured out what it's going to take to get over the next hurdle.

> *Only you have the power to understand yourself and where you want to go. Only you know if you really have what it takes to beat addiction down.*

The False "Cure" for Addiction

An awful lot of energy has gone into understanding the origins of addiction. These discoveries have lead to important insights—all of which have been essential to my life today and to my work advising and helping others. But the most glaring result of this research has been its collection of evidence of what *doesn't* work. And what doesn't work is almost everything we are doing.

As mentioned in Chapter 1, there is general agreement that only 10 percent of people with alcohol and drug problems get help in any structured way.[1] This tells us that the existing explanations and solutions are just not meeting the needs of the vast majority of people. The recommended treatment approaches are seen as too hard or foreign, the results too unappealing, and the failure rate too high.

In fact, the evidence that our current system is deeply failing us is so clear that it's simply scary no one has changed it yet. My own postdoctoral research focused on this indirectly and was the reason I left academia for more clinical and educational routes. I wanted to play a part in innovating new approaches and changing the outcomes for so many people who had failed or been left out of treatment.

Let's start with the fact that approximately 90 percent of those who struggle with addiction don't get treatment! There is no other known medical field where this proportion of people who are diagnosed with a condition choose *not to get treatment for it.* For comparison, when it comes to cancer, the statistic is essentially reversed, with approximately 10 percent of patients *not* getting a course of treatment after being diagnosed.[3]

> *Approximately 90 percent of those who struggle with addiction don't get treatment! There is no other known medical field where this proportion of people who are diagnosed with a condition choose not to get treatment for it.*

The rationale for this miserable rate of treatment has always been that addicts are lying, manipulative, sick people who are in denial of their own problem. But that's an incredibly misinformed and self-righteous way to look at a problem. It's like blaming people who keep walking out of your restaurant for having terrible taste in food as the reason your restaurant is not succeeding when the obvious answer it staring right at you—your food is terrible, your menu is overpriced, and your service is nonexistent.

The truth is staring us in the face: the addiction treatment system stinks. Most people don't want to take part in it, and those who do participate aren't getting anywhere near the help they need. And people are dying because of it. In fact, more people are dying from drugs and alcohol every year and the pace isn't slowing down.[4-6] Those who are not dying are still going to jail in much too high numbers[7,8]—despite some efforts to change policy—for a problem we are calling a chronic disease,[9] and no one wants to take the "medicine"—i.e., treatment—that is being offered for it.

We "buy into" the explanations and methods that fit us best, and we make do—even though we know there's something missing.

How have we gotten to this point when all the information is there for another way?

The Limits of Explanations

We've all heard the expression, "We don't know what we don't know." This point was brought home for me when I heard a NASA scientist answer the classic question at a press conference: "Do you think we'll find life on Mars?" The occasion was the launch of the Pathfinder satellite's twenty-year mission to Mars. His answer turned my thinking upside down.

He said something along the lines of, "We will look for life as we understand life—carbon-based molecules with external walls and an internal machinery. As long as the life we find on Mars looks like that, we should be able to identify it."

There was great humility in his answer and a recognition of a truth we rarely speak of: We only see what we know to look for. We don't know *what* we don't know. But the matter is even more complicated than that.

We only know to look for what we already understand, and we can only look for it where there's enough light—enough existing awareness, knowledge, and money—to do the search. This has been the history of humankind, and it's the reason behind so many significant revelations— from our realization that the gods on Mount Olympus do not exist, the earth is not shaped like a flat disc, and the planets orbit around the sun and not the earth to the existence of impossibly small microbes that can make us ill, and so much more.

We didn't know what we were looking for, and we didn't know where to look for it—until one illumination, one insight, and one leap of imagination led to the next breakthrough. We are always one revelation away from an incredible, life-altering discovery. We just don't know it until it becomes perfectly clear.

So what are the schools of thought that have shaped our collective ideas about recovery?

The Four Addiction "Camps": The State of Our Explanations

When it comes to addiction, the same story is true. We start with myths and move on to the trailblazers and pathfinders, looking for new and better answers. For hundreds of years the way we've looked at addiction has evolved as new information has come to light.

Unbeknownst to most of the general public, a war of sorts has been going on within the addiction field. The reason for this conflict? A struggle to uncover the *true* cause of addiction. Basically four main schools of thought have been battling for superiority. Each "camp" has aimed to identify *the* root cause for addiction and, by doing so, offer the best method to achieve a "cure" and eradicate it from our midst.

Given the sorrows and desperation that come with addiction, who wouldn't support that cause? Who wouldn't want to stem the tide of destruction that addiction causes? However, these good intentions contain an unintended consequence. With so many people involved and so much money being poured into—dare I say—the "addiction recovery industrial complex," how we define "success" and the "best" program and approach can come at the expense of the very people who are desperate for help. So, here are the camps—very broadly and simplistically identified—that have shaped our view of addiction and our understanding of "what's wrong" with the addict:

Camp #1: Spiritualists and Religionists

Camp #2: Psychotherapists and Traumatists

Camp #3. Neuroscientists and Biologists

Camp #4. Environmentalists and Social Scientists

To bring these unique vantage points out into the light, I'll provide simplified but, I hope, instructive explanations, progressing from the earliest to the most recent ones.

> *With so many people involved and so much money being poured into—dare I say—the "addiction recovery industrial complex," how we define "success" and the "best" program and approach can come at the expense of the very people who are desperate for help.*

Camp #1: The Spiritualists and Religionists

This camp is likely the oldest, going all the way back to the days when alcoholics and addicts were seen as being possessed by the devil. Exorcisms and baptisms were considered appropriate cures long ago.[10]

Although not quite as supernatural in their approach, today's spiritualists believe that individual difficulties such as addiction are actually a symptom of a spiritual void or malady. The absence of God (explicitly) or a Higher Power (more broadly) is seen as the underlying cause of addiction.[11] Get some more God-power inside, and He will take care of it (i.e., one of the most well-known AA phrases: "Let go and let God"). The solution is to engage in recovery approaches that get you closer to God, such as returning to or beginning a spiritual practice—Christian, Jewish, Muslim, Buddhist, or otherwise—or attending Twelve-Step meetings that provide their own system for spiritual support and growth.

I would argue that some addiction and policy experts who support criminal justice approaches to addiction—meaning they focus on drug use as an illegal activity and incarceration as an effective means to relieve the scourge from our midst—are actually part of this camp too.

Why? Because the underlying tenet is that bad people become addicted, and so bad people need to be punished for their sins. I mean, who would think of jailing a sick person with cancer or gallstones or a person injured by trauma or suffering from depression or bipolar disorder if they believed this to be the root cause of their trouble? But bad people get punished, and addicts are "bad" people, so addicts need to be punished.

The most popular self-help group out there—Alcoholics Anonymous—closely ties spirituality and a belief in "God" to recovery. The Alcoholics Anonymous book mentions the word *God* 134 times (281 times if other references to God are included),[12] and the group itself is often considered to be an extension of the earlier Oxford Groups, which were religious in nature.

There is, in fact, research evidence that links religious beliefs with differences in mental health and substance use patterns. Having stronger religious beliefs *and* more fundamentalist belief patterns does seem to predict less substance use.[13,14] Not surprisingly, AA members typically report significantly greater spiritual and religious leanings as compared to members of other groups that don't include God in their materials (such as SMART Recovery's model of volunteer mutual support groups).[15]

Unfortunately, research studies have generally shown that individuals with alcohol and drug problems tend to be somewhat more internally focused (believing less in external control).[16] That means they don't necessarily believe in a God with external power and authority, so as a group they are less likely to benefit from a recovery approach that is so reliant on faith in an outside force.

Camp #2. Psychotherapists and Traumatists

The Psychotherapists and Traumatists Camp looks at the subjective experience of the individual and the psychological impact that experience has on them. They start with the belief that any mental health struggle stems from a psychic conflict due to some previous experience. Resolving this psychic experience is the necessary component for relieving the problem. They don't have a problem incorporating spirituality into their approaches, but they see it as an element of an individual's interpretation of the world.

The many different techniques and schools of thought within this camp include psychoanalysis, cognitive behavioral therapy (CBT) interventions to change internal beliefs, Motivational Enhancement Therapy (MET), or trauma work to release built-in damage. People often use drugs to cope with difficulties—thus the casual references to "self-medicating" with drugs, alcohol, food, sex, or even video games.[17] We know that drug and alcohol problems often go together with mental health difficulties such as anxiety, depression, schizophrenia, and other conditions. It is estimated that about 60 percent of people with addiction problems also struggle with mental health issues.[1,18,19]

Not surprisingly, a substantial portion of individuals who enter treatment for substance use report having a history of trauma and/or mental health difficulties. Child abuse, violence, sexual trauma, and PTSD are some of the strongest and most reliable risk factors predicting the occurrence and greater severity of addiction later in life.[20,21]

In a National Institutes of Justice survey, teens who experienced physical or sexual abuse/assault were three times more likely to report past or current substance abuse than those without a history of trauma.[22] Estimates suggest that as many as 80 percent of women seeking treatment for drug abuse report lifetime histories of sexual and/or physical assault.[23] In veteran populations, PTSD has long been considered a substantial reason for increased substance use, as well as suicide, regardless of actual combat deployment.[24]

With a deep focus on talk therapy and cognitive exercises to understand one's experiences, release shame, and address trauma triggers and emotional overload, this camp utilizes powerful approaches to support recovery. But on its own, the Psychotherapists and Traumatists Camp can leave individuals without the potentially useful focus on environmental and biological forces possibly at play.

Camp #3. The Neuroscientists and Biologists

The biological explanation for addiction essentially states that we are predisposed to use and abuse substances (and engage in compulsive behavior) because of our genetic blueprint and the ways our brains are wired. Furthermore, in addition to the predispositions we might be born with, the use of substances triggers processes that change some of the most basic ways our brains work and further drive our craving for the addictive substance, cementing our addiction as near permanent.

According to the Neuroscientists and Biologists Camp, once an addiction is triggered there is, to date, no way to put the genie back in the bottle. This is a central component of the "addiction as a disease" model.[25] (The rather crude AA expression puts it this way, "You can't turn a pickle back to a cucumber.")

According to the biologists, everything can be explained by its inter-action with our body's mechanical systems—neurons and supporting cells in the brain and the rest of the nervous system; genes and epigenetic alter-ations throughout our cells; and the cardiovascular and endocrine systems that support it all".

At its core, the Neuroscientists and Biologists Camp believes that all the experiences you've had in life have shaped you because of the biological changes they've created in your body and brain. When your body and brain interact with the world, your biological reactions shape your behavior and thought. On the one hand, your biology makes it more likely that you will experience specific outcomes, and on the other hand, your interactions with the world cement your fate through biological changes. Ultimately, this camp believes that when individuals engage in problematic behavior, something about their biology has gone awry.

For example, some people may be more predisposed to anxiety, depres-sion, or addiction regardless of what happens to them in the world.[26,27] But if their environment and experiences in the world cause additional stress to the biological system, their mental health condition might worsen.[28-30] When it comes to addiction, the alcohol or drug use hijacks your brain's mechanisms and drives additional drug use through a whole chain of bio-logical interactions.[31] Many people understand the addicted brain to be inherently different than a "regular" brain by using the analogy of a switch being thrown between the two. Once the switch has been thrown, you can't reverse it.[25,32] But extensive scientific evidence simply does not support this conclusion.

For instance, research on Vietnam veterans, who used large amounts of heroin while fighting overseas, found that many of them stopped their heavy heroin use once they returned home.[33] And research from the National Institute on Alcohol Abuse and Alcoholism (NIAAA) has revealed that fully 75 percent of individuals who struggle with alcohol at one point in life are found to recover later, with some struggling for only about four years and others for an average of twenty years.[34,35] These findings fly in the face of the addiction theories of the time and still run counter to our popular understanding of addiction.

Consider what this means. If biology triggers permanent dependence, and we know heroin dependence is one of the toughest to beat, then many more soldiers would have continued using after deployment, and alcoholics would stay alcoholics forever.

The Neurologists and Biologists Camp supposes that people abuse alcohol and drugs only because of the way the chemicals affect the brain. Different drugs affect the system differently, but dopamine release has been implicated in the increased motivation to use alcohol and drugs.[31] Essentially, all addictive substances (and behaviors) increase dopamine release one way or another.[36]

As evidence, many studies have shown that by blocking dopamine activity (and more recently opiates), people (and animals) use less drugs.[37-39] In the case of opiates, substances that do a "better" or more efficient job of activating opioid receptors tend to have better pain impact, but are also more likely to be abused.[40] Repeated substance use causes long-term, if not permanent, alterations in some of the most basic reward systems in the addict's brain when compared to "nonaddicts."[32,41,42]

This same research has sometimes led to a deterministic, fixed, understanding of addiction, but it's also led to research on the effectiveness of pharmacological treatments (medication) in helping people overcome their problems with alcohol and drug use, including withdrawal, cravings, managing emotional effects of trauma, and addressing co-occurring mental health difficulties.[43-45] Our understanding of biology has also helped the development of techniques such as biofeedback,[46] which helps counter or even reverse some of the effects of substance use, and EMDR,[47] a technique to process traumatic memories. Researchers also are working on vaccines[48] to block drug use all together, hoping that chemical intervention would suffice.

Brain imaging studies, one of the standout techniques used by neuro-scientists, have revealed substantial differences in the activation patterns that "addicts" and "nonaddicts" show.[49,50] Studies have also shown us that repeated drug use can compromise learning, potentially making it more difficult to change behavior (such as stopping problematic drug use).[51,52] Studies of twins and more statistically advanced (and recent) genetics research reveal a substantial amount of genetic contribution to the risk for developing addiction problems that can range from 30 to 60 percent.[53] Some studies suggest this variation in genetic contribution is related to the specific substance being used, while other studies show the variability is associated with gender or other related factors.[54-56]

However, "risk factor" is not destiny. My clients and students find it enormously helpful to understand the powerful role of biology—as well as its limits. Biology and genes can suggest a tendency or potential reality. But the research also proves that biology is not static. We have the ability within ourselves to shape our futures, and tools are available to help us accomplish that, which many people are happy and relieved to utilize when appropriate.

Camp #4. Environmentalists and Social Scientists

Unlike the tree-hugging variety, environmentalists in the addiction war believe that external factors and forces dictate the behavior of the organisms within it.

Indeed, this camp believes that the rules and standards of a particular society (the environment) and the way that society defines the problem creates the addiction and therefore creates the view of those who struggle within it.[57,58] Stressful environments create stress, which affects people and alters their behavior. Lifting that stress changes behavior again and works to alleviate the problem that had manifested itself. Environmentalists typically belong to the social psychology or sociology disciplines and look at the systems that exist outside of a person to explain the drivers of behavior.

For example, we know that drinking rates increase substantially and substance use prevalence rates peak for teens as they enter young adulthood (ages eighteen to twenty-four).[59] The environmental effect of lots of young people socializing together is greatest in universities and is further magnified within Greek organizations where alcohol and drug consumption is especially high and a focal point of activity.[60,61] People drink more when those around them drink more, and studies have shown that greater "peer-pressure" susceptibility in adolescence is linked to greater substance use.[62]

Another environmental factor is our very understanding of what constitutes "problematic" drug and alcohol consumption. In fact, drinking standards in the US have changed drastically over the past two hundred years. Drinking averages as much as five times the current standard were the norm back in colonial times.[63] Current moderation standards call for one to fourteen weekly drinks for a man; greater drinking quantities qualify as "heavy drinking."[64] Substantially more drinking would have been both acceptable and expected in the eighteenth century. Laws and regulations, in addition to public standards, set the guidelines for what is considered "deviant," "problematic," and illegal (as with drunk driving). As those standards change, behavior that was once acceptable can be redefined as "troubled."

One of the strongest environmental influences early on in life has to do with familial interactions, and parenting styles have long been shown to affect substance use patterns, with specific styles (i.e., authoritative parenting) linked to reductions in risk and others, such as authoritarian or avoidant, potentially leading to increased mental health difficulties, including substance use.[65]

Environmentalists are often less clear, as a group, about what will relieve addiction problems. This is especially so since some argue that addiction itself is a made-up concept. While some focus on the elimination of laws that criminalize drugs, other focus on the reconceptualization of addiction itself in order to remove the focus from the individual.

I find the environmental perspective most helpful in leading clients to see how powerful their surroundings, community, relationship, and even their home can lead toward health or toward relapse. While we take it for granted, our environment has an incredibly strong influence on our behavior and the ways we see the world.

Joining Together: Why We Need to Embrace All the Explanations

Each of the four addiction camps has had the benefit of brilliant minds who have developed its theories and propagated its methods for recovery. Each of these camps has provided incredible insights into the problem of addiction using research, clinical evidence, and anecdotal experiences. And each has enjoyed a period of time in the sunny fields of public opinion. Throughout the evolution of these theories, the mythology of addiction has evolved along with them. The explanations, stories, images, and archetypes we recognize and believe today are based on these distinct yet overlapping worldviews.

Depending on what we've learned and experienced ourselves, most of us will find ourselves more aligned with one camp or another—and they all have value. In fact, each of these camps appreciates, to some extent, the explanations offered by the others. The fight is simply about which factor matters the most.

The National Institute on Drug Abuse (NIDA) and the biologists recognize that environmental influence matters. The environmentalists agree that if drugs didn't have a biological impact, they wouldn't be used. Those who are psychologically oriented realize that without social pressure from the environment, there would be less problematic use. But in general, the overriding sentiment is that if *their* camp's explanation were fully recognized, it would trump all other needs for the reason behind addiction.

However, confirmation bias continues driving participants in each of these camps toward their own corners:

* The spiritualists regard everyone else as missing the point when they seek material, worldly explanations for an impossible-to-understand, supranatural reality.

* Those who believe that trauma and the psychological experiences are the true culprits recognize that neuroscience has explanations of internal processes related to thought and behavior, but they believe it is simply the explanation of *how* a machine works and not the reason (or fuel) behind *why* it does.

* The biologists interpret childhood trauma through the lens of the impact it has on biology (the HPA axis and its role in our stress response).

* And the environmentalists look at the dopamine system as a normal part of biological functioning and relegate the biologists' explanation of its role in addiction as a socially informed manipulation of normal behavior into deviant explanations.

Thus we end up with environmentalists and biologists mocking spiritual pursuits as a solution. The spirit-seekers look down on those who utilize medical approaches in addition to, or instead of, psychological or spiritual fixes. It's good intentions at their worst as everyone tries to beat the others into submission.

But as we fight for "who's right," millions suffer, often in silence. They don't have a voice in this fight. In the crisis of addiction, people primarily get help for the aspect of their addiction that fits the belief of their provider: spiritual (Twelve-Step meetings, prayers, and sermons). psychological (talk and behavior modification therapy), biological (medication), or environmental (assistance and support).

And the approach rarely incorporates the individual's personal experience (because addicts are liars who can't be trusted and are in denial anyway). To make matters worse, the vast majority of treatment in the United States is stuck in a strange limbo between purely spiritual (through AA indoctrination) and abstractly biological (with weak but increasing adoption of medication).

The shocking truth is: a single explanation can never fully illuminate a problem as complex as addiction, and there is rarely a single method for recovery—or even a single definition of recovery, as well see.

People Are Not Fixed— Nor Is Addiction

For many people, there remains a nagging and essential question of whether addiction is a biological disease that originates from a sort of allergy to alcohol (Alcoholics Anonymous' language), a brain disease (as the National Institute on Drug Abuse calls it), or a personal choice made by social deviants who are selfish and uncaring.

Until very recently the entire "addiction" definition rested on the notion that there were "normal" people and "addicts." All of us were either one or the other—but never both.

However, what if "addiction" isn't one thing? What if addiction is a syndrome—a set of symptoms that show themselves similarly even if the underlying reasons for their development are very different?

What if 'addiction' is a syndrome- a set of symptoms that show themselves similarly even if the underlying reasons for their development are very different?

If we step away from the reflection of our ideas in the mirror (a Pygmalion effect of sorts, seeing our concept mirrored back to us), we might discover that addiction fits all these explanations, whether we see it as a made-up response to a stressful and troubling society, a biologically determined disease, a moral and spiritual void, or a response to traumatic childhood experiences. We *may* just find out that it can be all of them.

Sometimes biology might be the primary culprit, while at other times environmental exposure might wield the power. Some people may have the genetics deck piled high against them, which may be magnified by early childhood trauma (including oxygen loss during the birth process itself and life-threatening illnesses) that can alter the biological machine.

For others, a social group in which drug use is incredibly common and ever-present may counter the impact of supportive parents and a biologically "clean" rap sheet. Spiritual pursuits may provide a fix for some, while medication or therapy does the trick for others because the underlying reasons are not the same. A complex presentation like "addiction" may require a complex explanation.

In fact, just as multiple factors explain the origins of addictions and routes for recovery, multiple factors are also at play in its actual progression. The mythology of addiction has led most of us to understand addiction as a disease that gets progressively worse until a person recovers—or dies. But there is another model.

Experience and research actually tells us that addiction doesn't have to be an acute *or* a chronic condition. For as many as 75 percent of people who struggle with alcohol, for instance, a problematic pattern of use holds for only a limited time period—in fact, four years or less on average. For others, the problem is much more persistent and pervasive, lasting for fifteen to twenty years or more.[34,35] Within this latter group some struggle continuously, while others move in and out of "addictive periods" throughout some part of their lives.

Whether an individual follows a treatment program, avoids treatment, or goes in and out of treatment, we know a substantial universe of people struggle for varying amounts of time. We've typically explained this phenomenon as the journey to hitting bottom. But that explanation only makes sense in hindsight, when one's problems have been resolved. Indeed, the same reasoning is sometimes used for withholding help until someone gets "bad enough" to be willing to engage in the treatment offered. Only then will the person truly submit to treatment, so this thinking goes.

If people can have a different mix of causes, it makes sense that the impact of each of these causes could change with time as well. As factors become more—or less—problematic, the overall severity of addiction waxes and wanes, and different types of recovery and different tools may be more or less helpful, depending on the stage of life or phase of addiction.

You see, addiction is not at all an either/or problem—it's a yes/and problem. We need *more* explanations, *more* solutions, and *more* acceptance of multiple paths to change and lead healthy lives.

The Myth of Sustained Abstinence as a Cure

Our focus on primary or single causes is compounded by our faith in a single solution. We have bought into the collective belief that abstinence is the only cure—abstinence now, forever, and completely. The "addiction recovery industrial complex" measures success in treatment by the percentage of clients abstinent a month, six-months, or a year after treatment, as if this singular yardstick is the be-all and end-all of success.

And success rates are dismal. Depending on what studies you believe and what population you pay attention to, current treatment success rates are between 10 and 35 percent—not exactly something to brag about[66] and no better than the rate of improvement among those who don't enter treatment.[34] The sort of success rates you hear in marketing materials for the biggest treatment organizations are essentially pure fiction. Programs regularly tout 70 percent success rates and higher with no scientific rigor behind them and no transparency.

But it's more than unsubstantiated claims. Research studies have repeatedly shown that a substantial proportion of participants in these studies actually lie about their abstinence. Numerous studies have shown that when comparing self-reported substance use to biological tests (such as breathalyzers or drug tests), people substantially underreport their use.[67,68]

One recent study found that, while 97 percent of participants actually consumed alcohol (as measured by an ankle sweat monitor), only 30 to 40 percent reported doing so.[69] This shows us that, in reality, nearly all treatment participants drink during treatment, and the vast majority lie about it when asked—even when they know they're being monitored. The social pressure of having to look good means that many people aren't honest about their slips. We have created a system where people can't be honest with their supposed helpers, and that sets up a terrible starting place for a therapeutic relationship.

Given the shame involved in telling someone that you've failed at reaching the goal of treatment—abstinence—it's no wonder so many lie.

But this doesn't surprise me in the least. Given the shame involved in telling someone that you've failed at reaching the goal of treatment—abstinence—it's no wonder so many lie. Indeed, asking a former client the question 'Are you sober?' can result in what researchers call a social desirability bias, whereby those who respond feel obliged to give the therapist or treatment center (where they spent a lot of time and money) the answer they know is being sought: "Yes."[70]

Obviously, we're missing something big here, and most treatment centers would rather not admit it.

At least one of the things we're missing is this: success, or recovery, is only partially related to abstinence. The Substance Abuse and Mental Health Services Administration (SAMHSA), the office dedicated to improving mental health and addiction in the US, defines recovery as:

A process of change through which individuals improve their health and wellness, live self-directed lives, and strive to reach their full potential.

SAMHSA's definition of recovery doesn't include abstinence anywhere within it. In fact, I tell those I work with that if all they achieved by working with me is abstinence, then I have failed them. True recovery is not about abstaining, but about flourishing.

So why is it that we've put all our focus on abstinence? I believe it is possible, and maybe even advisable, to help those who struggle in the areas that *they* are most interested in focusing on. I've found that when we take this approach, resistance to treatment nearly disappears. Why do we feel the need to create hurdles so high for people dealing with addiction?

Nearly everyone who struggles with addiction knows they need help; they just might not want help with the specific aspect of their struggle that everyone else wants to help them with—namely abstinence.

> *True recovery is not about abstaining, but about flourishing.*

For those who struggle with psychological difficulties, environmental stressors, or crumbling relationships, like Terry from our story, the resolution or improvement of those other areas of life can often be the impetus for so much additional change. But by making abstinence the guard at the gate, we keep most of those who need help outside, when all it would take is the simple extension of a helping hand. By making abstinence the de facto standard for recovery, we keep more people sick than we help.

So here we are—in the middle of a war about who's right regarding the core underlying reasons for addiction. It's a war with battles being won by different factions at different time points but it includes millions of people as collateral damage. This ridiculous war is *the* reason for the terrible death toll and financial costs associated with addiction—just as much as the addiction problem itself. Because we have a system that provides terrible outcomes and that no one wants to participate in, millions of people are suffering needlessly and dying, or getting sick, or ending up in prisons.

It's time to stop fighting. It's time for a new way forward.

EXERCISE: *Exploring the Explanations That Fit YOU*

No matter how dogmatic others have been about the "true" cause for addiction, you've likely always felt something was missing from the equation. You've always known that the truth is not quite as simple as others have tried to persuade you it is.

If you dig in and step back, what is the unique combination of factors—from your biological and psychological makeup, your current and past environment, and your spiritual connection—that has led you to this place?

This work can be helped greatly by the guidance of a professional, but you already have much of this information within you, even if it's been ignored or devalued. Knowing that an examination of all this information can reveal the exact nature of your struggles, what factors would you put on the table?

1. Biology

   a. Record the names of relations who have struggled with addiction themselves.

   b. Identify early-life struggles with anxiety, depression, impulsivity, or other personality traits.

   c. Record any health issues, physical injuries, or accidents that may have contributed to your addiction (examples include complications at birth, head injuries, severe pain leading to medication dependence, and other circumstances).

2. Psychology

   a. List any important life experiences that may have caused trauma.

   b. Did your early relationships support your self-esteem and agency (the belief in your ability to accomplish things) or damage it?

3. Environment

   a. Was your initial use of substances affected by external social pressures and/or internally motivated factors?

   b. Do you currently use to overcome social anxiety or to fit in?

   c. What proportion of your social group includes heavy substance users?

4. Spirituality

   a. Do you see your life as being controlled by your actions or by an external force or being?

   b. Would you identify yourself as religious?

    i. If so, to what extent are you engaged in spiritual pursuits?

    ii. If not, is this a source of anxiety or a sense of loss for you?

5. What insights regarding your struggles has this exercise revealed to you that weren't clear when you began reading this chapter?

CHAPTER 5

A NEW MODEL OF RECOVERY

Three Principles and Nine Steps
to Your Personalized Plan

Ｔrue recovery isn't about abstinence or sticking with a recovery program. True recovery is about getting to a point where you are attending to—and expanding—the direction of your life. Indeed, I would say that anyone struggling with addiction has ignored whole areas of their life for some time—whether it's their health, career, relationships, self-improvement, sense of purpose, or being a contributing member of society.

This more comprehensive concept of recovery is something I've seen work for hundreds of people in my own practice. It is supported by my own research on why people actually seek help (for a better life) and why they might avoid it. It is also consistent with recent findings on why, for many who do seek help, the offered solutions (treatment and recovery approaches) rarely match their purpose or needs.

Searching for a Recovery Path That Fits

One client, John, recently explained it to me this way:

> I was desperate to save my marriage and I literally willed myself to stop using. I went to four therapists and stuck with ten months of treatment and meetings. I managed to keep clean, but even in that sobriety, I never understood how I got to such a bad place. I kept having this obsessive question about why I was acting out.

> The answer I kept hearing did nothing to help me. Everyone told me I was an addict and a liar and I'd always be that way. If I were lucky, my solution would be to work really hard so I could be a sober addict and a liar. I hated that mind-set. It made me feel broken and worthless. I hated the idea that no matter how long I was sober, I'd always be less than other people. I'd never be free of the burden of addiction.

> Since I've started to learn about a broader concept of recovery, it hasn't made things easier, but it has given me amazing sense of possibility. I don't have to be an addict. I can face my fears, my experiences, and not be ashamed. I can face them and grow.

> As I've started looking at my life, I've started to see that my addiction was born from the isolation and lack of intimacy I experienced as a child. My addiction became a crutch to deal with those experiences, and I developed a dangerous cycle of using my addiction and driving myself into further isolation out of fear of people knowing how damaged I was. I never knew how deep those emotions ran or the effect they still had on my life.

> I don't have all the answers yet, but I am finally understanding and accepting where I am. I'm realizing I can confront and deal with the underlying issues that have contributed to my addiction and the shame I've always done everything to avoid. This new

perspective is giving me a powerful sense of relief. It's inspired me to want to work harder, dig deeper, and look directly at the points of pain because I know I want to confront them in order to have the life I want.

I'm having new conversations with my wife, and she has a new sense of possibility for our life together too. The feeling of hope I've gained has been the greatest gift I've ever received.

Truth Is a Catalyst

John's hope and new perspective for recovery is also what I know from my own search for help.

When I was so disconnected from normal life, when I was using and dealing and living the fast life in LA, when I was constantly seeking any new rush to keep my terrible thoughts about myself at bay, when I was cut off from my family to avoid my shame and theirs, no area of my life was really on the right track.

My life seemed highly functional from the outside. I'd managed to graduate from college. I had two cars, a motorcycle, a fancy apartment, and a rented recording studio. But if you looked any deeper, you'd have seen that everything was slowly rotting. I felt stuck, depressed, and hopeless that things would ever get better. Any single moment I spent alone was full of self-doubt and depression. I was hopelessly dependent on the drugs I was using (for money and comfort). Music wasn't getting me anywhere (I'd originally moved to LA to pursue my dreams of being a musician). I couldn't stand the way I felt even for five seconds, which meant I needed to use all the time. I was just upping the ante on blotting out my future.

And then I got arrested, and I substituted the drama of the criminal justice system for the drama of addiction. Being arrested and having my life upended was painful, but it led to the first good thing to happen in a long time. It was a relief to have everyone know what was actually going on.

*Being arrested and having my life upended
was painful, but it led to the first good
thing to happen in a long time. It was a
relief to have everyone know what was
actually going on.*

While I was fighting my case, I went to rehab at my lawyer's recommendation. I knew I was addicted to meth, but rehab seemed extreme—until my attorney told me that unless I spent some serious time in treatment, I would likely spend somewhere between ten and twenty years in prison.

So off to rehab I went. I experienced the most traditional version of treatment imaginable. It was based on the Twelve Steps, with daily AA meetings and the expectation of a life lived as an addict in recovery forever. I couldn't stand it.

Within two months, I received permission to go back to work. For me, "work" was essentially free time hanging out in my recording studio in downtown LA and playing around—and dealing. Of course I went back to meth. Even after two months of being sober, it was just so natural. I found some in my studio and used a little right away, saving the rest for later. But within days I was back to using it daily. It took a few more weeks for me to get caught. I was immediately kicked out of rehab; zero tolerance was the name of the game.

It was terrible and a relief all at once. The hardest part was the phone call with my dad, which was about to turn into another piece of evidence that I was a no-good-piece-of-*$&%.

Almost.

It started out with me calling him to let him know I had moved out of rehab. At first the conversation went exactly as I wanted it to. He was buying my story—that the rehab was too far from my work and I needed to be back in Los Angeles, not all the way out in Pasadena. He was buying everything I was selling, just as everyone always had.

But then something switched inside me. I heard a little voice that said, "Just tell him the truth."

You see, I wasn't planning on moving anywhere. I had tried lying to the rehab managers, too, but they wouldn't accept anything I said. I was out on the street, homeless (or living in my car). I screwed up, and I had to pay the price.

I wanted to find a way to save face with my father. He'd put so much faith, money, and effort into helping me, and I didn't want him to know the truth. But then I did it. I just blurted it out. I told him what had actually happened. I felt a bowling ball lodged in my stomach. It was hard to breathe; I started crying. But somehow I got the words out.

My dad started yelling at me. He was so mad. He couldn't understand how I would screw up something this important, something that could land me in prison for nearly twenty years. He said, "What the hell do you want me to do now?"

I had no idea how I could screw it up either, but I knew it was up to me to figure it out. It was the first time I stopped my lying—to myself and everyone else. Telling my dad was cathartic.

In that moment, the bowling ball disappeared from my stomach. I caught my breath, stopped crying, and answered him. "You can't do anything about this. I have to figure it out. It's up to me to fix it."

Quitting meth became, for the first time, not about quitting meth but rather about proving to myself that I could do what was necessary to stay in treatment and not get kicked out. I had tried to quit four or five times before, but my goal never went past a belief that said, "I don't have to use today; I can make it to tomorrow without using."

For a couple of weeks, while I looked for my next rehab, I continued using. But something inside me had changed. I couldn't avoid the truth I knew inside. I still faked things on the outside for a while—such as continuing to sell drugs when I was at my lawyer's office—but I was also making changes, and I couldn't deal with that level of self-deceit anymore. Once you see behind the curtain, it gets harder to un-see.

There were many occasions over the following year that previously would have led me to storm out, quit, start lying, or tell everyone to fuck off. But with my new resolve, I found that each situation gave me practice in simply sticking it out through difficult times. Gradually I improved my relationship with my family (I started answering their calls and letting them know what was really going on), my health (I started working out), my mind (I started reading and going to movies and enjoying life), and my sense of purpose (I now saw my well-being tied connected to my family's, and I wanted to remove myself as a source of pain for them).

With those things at the forefront of my mind, quitting meth proved much easier. I fought my terrible habits and my boredom and my criminal case—not using meth. Using meth didn't even seem attractive any longer (although those pesky cravings would come out of nowhere sometimes). I ended up spending eight months in that final rehab before the dreaded day in court when my future would be decided.

I risked a guilty plea as my best shot at avoiding a long prison sentence. I had done all the work, gotten completely sober, and gratefully, the Honorable Judge Fox sentenced me to only one year in jail. At the sentencing, the judge made it clear that he was giving me this opportunity because he truly believed in my desire to change. He also hung seven years over my head in case I messed up. I was determined not to.

Once I completed my year of hell (and there are more than enough stories to go with it), with my father visiting as often as he could (my mom and sister couldn't bear it), I regained my freedom. I flew back to Israel for my first visit in over five years. Life started feeling very different.

Over time, the work I was doing to improve my life became the foreground of what mattered to me. My recovery became the background that allowed all kinds of wonderful new things to happen—getting into graduate school at UCLA, meeting the woman who would become my wife, developing a circle of friends who reminded me of my childhood back in Tel Aviv. I was happy—not every day, but most of the time. I was grateful for everything I had, and I looked forward the future ahead of me.

Challenging the Barriers to Treatment

Everyone experiences challenges on the path of recovery, but it took me a long time to see that many of the barriers to treatment were systemic— not personal.

My ideas about the problems with our treatment system began to take shape once I received my PhD in psychology from UCLA and joined their Integrated Substance Abuse Programs (ISAP), a collection of cutting-edge centers dealing with addiction research, training, and treatment. I'd been conducting research on the neuroscience of addiction, using rats to study the body's response to drugs and their impact on the brain. But now I wanted to turn my attention from the causes and processes of addiction to the processes of treatment.

That's when I discovered the fact that only 10 percent of individuals with alcohol or drug problems enroll in treatment. I was shocked. There were no other conditions I knew of that showed this sort of resistance to getting help. Obviously, I wanted to figure out why. I was surprised to discover how little research existed on the topic, so I did what any scientist would do—I designed my own study.

The little research that was available (conducted in the 1990s by John Cunningham and Linda and Mark Sobell) showed surprising reasons why people didn't go into treatment. They weren't in denial of their problem. Instead:

* They were embarrassed and ashamed.

- They felt stigmatized and unable to share their problems.

- They held negative attitudes about the treatments that were available.

These explanations sounded completely different from the stories and messages I'd heard and believed. Even after my own experience in treatment and ten years of education in psychology, I bought into the myths and explanations that addicts who didn't seek help are lazy, unmotivated, selfish liars who are in denial.[71] Like most people, I believed addicts didn't care about anyone else but themselves and, due to changes in their brains, were willing to do anything to keep drinking or using. I'm sure you've had these beliefs too.

The results of my study replicated the earlier findings by Cunningham. However, we followed our participants for six months (whereas the Cunningham study was based on a one-time assessment), and we learned a lot along the way. Several new findings came to the forefront:

- Shame became less of an issue. Over the months of the study, our participants experienced substantial reductions in reported shame, even though many were still not engaging in formal treatment.

- Costs and logistics seemed to be bigger problems than had earlier been found, a fact that wasn't being discussed in the research world where most treatment is publicly funded. This made sense. While insurance covered most costs of treatment in the 1980s and early 1990s, treatment in the decades that followed became increasingly expensive, costing between five thousand and fifty thousand dollars a month. (I know families that have spent hundreds of thousands of dollars and have gone into debt while their loved one is still struggling.)

Treatment can also take up a lot of time, requiring individuals to commit to thirty days or more away from their life for residential programs (you try taking thirty to ninety days away from all of your responsibilities and still keep your job) or at least ten hours per week for more local outpatient treatment. Those two factors mean a lot of for anyone.

And there was one more answer that jumped out at us:

- About 50 percent of the respondents agreed "strongly" or "very strongly" with the statement: "I enjoy drinking/drug use too much to stop," and said this was a reason for them to delay or avoid treatment.

This was strange, because the study was solely designed for people seeking addiction treatment. In fact, people were only admitted to the study through a website I had started to help people access treatment for their addiction struggles. The study participants indicated that they had either entered, or were still seeking, help throughout their participation.

So what was going on? Everyone knew that to get treatment you had to be willing to stop using.

When I first began presenting our research, I kept hearing feedback that the participants who reported they enjoyed using too much to stop must not "really be interested in treatment." But the data didn't show that. We knew from the study that those same people had looked for help before—and were looking for help now.

My interpretation was completely different from the scientists and addiction experts who were giving me feedback. I believed that the study participants wanted help and knew they *needed* help—even though they enjoyed using too much to stop. Their ambivalence didn't mean they were unmotivated or uninterested.

That's when it dawned on me that the key word in that option was *stop*. It's the word everyone I knew in the addiction field had simply taken for granted. What if this word was the cause of the confusion? What if people wanted help, but they just didn't want to stop? And what if that was okay?

What if people wanted help, but they just didn't want to stop?

The idea seemed revolutionary and, indeed, when spoken out loud, most people simply scoffed at it.

Have you ever mentioned to anyone that you were trying to cut back, only to be looked at sideways? Has any therapist or helper ever told you that it's impossible and simply dismiss you offhand? Then you know what I mean.

Everyone knows addicts and alcoholics can only succeed in life if they completely abstain from any and all "mind altering substances." The idea is simple: Addicts are different from other people. Whether the basis is genetics, a biological switch, a spiritual malady, or a psychological trauma or vulnerability, they are either born with, or are altered into, a state of being where they cannot control their substance use.

The primary schools of thought and all the prevailing treatment approaches all agree on one thing—addicts have to be abstinent to be successful. And it makes sense. When addicts are using, they usually bring about some pretty terrible suffering (at least for everyone else around them).

There were only two problems, as far as I could see.

First, requiring "abstinence first" was one of the major hurdles people reported that kept them out of treatment. People who were not ready to quit everything were deemed not serious about getting help, and thus there was nothing we could do for them.

A person can be begging for help but not yet ready to quit everything, and treatment center after treatment center will turn them away. Many clients have told me about therapists who wouldn't see them until they had been clean for thirty days. That's a little like asking a cancer patient to heal themselves before you see them (if you believe in the disease theory, which these practitioners all did).

Second, requiring "permanent abstinence" or else assuming the person is doomed to relapse over and over again is often not true. In fact, many people don't follow this pattern.[72,73] This second problem was more personal for me. I had been a meth addict and, as I was conducting this research, I was back to drinking socially without a problem. Sure, whenever I wrote about it, I got incredible pushback. People told me that sharing my story (with all the obvious signs that I'm a relapsing addict) "will kill other addicts."

I didn't expect the findings of the study I led, and initially I didn't know what to do with them. I had been free of all mind-altering substances for three whole years myself. It was the only thing anyone told me was possible. But here I was, an ex-addict who was able to drink socially, finding out there are potentially millions of people who would get help tomorrow if they weren't asked to commit to quitting—now and forever—before they even began their recovery.

That's when I decided to leave the comfort of the ivory tower and begin bringing about change in the way treatment was administered.

A New Entry Point for Recovery

To me, we clearly needed a path to recovery that was wide open- where everyone could seek and receive help and without abstinence as the prerequisite and only measure of success.

Clearly we needed a path to recovery that was wide open—where everyone could seek and receive help and without abstinence as the prerequisite and only measure of success.

After more than seven years of research, including the UCLA study of how and when people seek help, my readings and exposure to harm-reduction literature and experts (such as Dr. Andrew Tatarsky and Dee-Dee Stout, among others), my individual work with hundreds of clients navigating the addiction world, curriculum development for educational programs (including the groundbreaking work of Dr. Stanton Peele and Dr. Allan Marlatt), and five years running a recovery center that aimed to do things differently, the IGNTD Recovery approach starts with a fresh set of premises based on the *reality* of what works rather than what we wish worked.

Premise #1: Eliminate abstinence as a barrier for receiving help.

The way I see it, if approximately 50 percent of the people who need and want help are balking at or avoiding treatment altogether because of the abstinence requirement, then it makes no sense to keep it around.

We tried versions of this approach at the treatment center I co-founded and led for five years, but IGNTD Recovery now takes it a step further. People need to be able to get help at whatever level they are willing to receive it.

To be clear, this does not mean that abstinence isn't important. Ironically, a good portion of clients who come to me looking for help in reducing their substance use (mostly for alcohol) have found they actually prefer abstinence. The point is simply this: abstinence shouldn't be a requirement for engaging in help.

Premise #2: A single solution will never be good enough.

In the previous chapter on the explanations for addiction, we looked at why each of the four camps has relevant arguments for the reasons for addiction:

- Drugs change the brain (biology).

- People use drugs to cope with difficulty and trauma (psychology).

- When in Rome, you drink like the Romans (environment).

- People who are devout seem to have fewer drug and alcohol problems (spirituality).

However, no matter how true these generalizations might be, they simply can't produce a satisfactory solution for everyone who struggles with addiction. The reason is the basis for the IGNTD Recovery approach. Each person has a unique combination of environmental, psychological, biological, and spiritual factors that create their current situation.

And you already knew this! That's why every time someone talks to you about addiction, it feels like *some* of what they say fits you perfectly and some simply doesn't make sense. If you try to say no to the explanations you receive, you're almost always told that you're in denial or you don't realize how serious the problem really is. But you aren't in denial. You simply recognize something is missing—the individual piece of the puzzle.

Premise #3. Addiction is not static.

The individual nature of addiction has another level that affects our experiences: addiction problems ebb and flow.

The way people talk about addiction, you'd think that addicts are always stuck in an incomprehensible mess of a life. But for many, that is simply not true. The different elements involved— spirituality, psychology, biology, and the environment—wax and wane in severity as people's lives change. As they get in and out of marriages or romantic relationships, surround themselves with different people, get sicker and healthier, face increased or reduced stress, and more, their addiction problem gets bigger or smaller—or disappears for long periods of time.

The reality is that most people float in and out of their "addiction" state, but for the most part no one is paying attention when the problem isn't there. Then all the old stories of addiction replay themselves when the person begins to struggle, perhaps after the death of a loved one, a job loss, or some other turning point.

No matter what cycle of addiction we might fit into, without a strong enough foundation, we may return to unhealthy behaviors when a crisis comes along, not because our disease was waiting in the wings, but because of our unique mix of strengths and vulnerabilities. Our lives have changed substantially and we may need help righting ourselves at that particular moment in our lives. What's more, what worked in the past may not work in the present.

> *No matter what cycle of addiction we might fit into, without a strong enough foundation, we may return to unhealthy behaviors when a crisis comes along. What's more, what worked in the past may not work in the present.*

The "problems" underlying our addictions are not constant and neither are the solutions. We can think of the analogy of someone diagnosed with cancer. The five stages of cancer describe the condition in terms of scale and impact from small and very localized to larger and beginning to spread, and finally to large and affecting multiple organs. Along the continuum there are different treatment approaches—including surgery, radiation, chemotherapy, plasma transfusions, and immunotherapy—and different prognoses. Some types of cancers and treatments even allow a person to control the disease's progression for many years, not by eradicating it but by managing it. It's similar to the model used for HIV infection, where a combination of drug therapies allows many people to live healthy lives without ever developing AIDS.

With addiction, people travel between the different severities and dysfunction all the time. We don't yet know:

1. How many people could "recover" completely

2. How many people could maintain long—perhaps lifelong—periods of occasional social use without any interference in their lives

3. How many people might be able to manage their addictive risks with self-knowledge, treatment methods, and long-term techniques—with or without abstinence

As long as we make it taboo to admit anything but the abstinence version of success, we'll never know.

"A Successful Life Cast with a Dark Shadow"—Julia's Story

Julia had tried everything she could think of before she came to me. She was a successful married professional in her early fifties. She was also motivated. Heavy drinking had been a part of her life for decades and was the one area of her life she hadn't taken control of. That's what she explained when we both sat down in front of our computers for our initial evaluation session. She had reached out because she knew I had experience with something called The Sinclair Method, a medication-supported approach to addiction treatment. I'd helped a few friends of hers, so she was somewhat optimistic, though she had tried so many treatment approaches over the years that she wasn't holding her breath. She was skeptical but hopeful—my favorite type of client.

Julia's Downward Spiral

Julia went to amazing schools and earned a BA and an MBA before entering the corporate world. She married and settled into a comfortable life, though she never truly stopped to think about her partying. It was a way of blowing off steam and letting her hair down when the rest of the time she felt she needed to be in control and always "on." She gave herself permission to celebrate her successes, more wildly in her twenties and thirties and a little less so in her forties, but still, partying was fun. . . until Julia decided she wanted to slow down. Midlife, drugs, and alcohol were not a great mix for her. The older she got, the more lethargic, depressed, and "heavy" she felt. She needed more rest and more downtime to keep up with the pace of her work and the big goals she still hoped to achieve.

Removing drugs from the equation was relatively easy for Julia, but the alcohol stuck around. She tried small breaks (with her husband's support)—one-week, then two, and even a whole month at one point. But then, inevitably, she would drink as heavily as before, if not more so, as soon as alcohol was on the menu again. Julia had tried therapy and self-help meetings a handful of times. The former helped, but not enough, while the latter simply made her run the other way. She felt lost. And she felt out of control.

That's when she heard about The Sinclair Method, which uses naltrexone to lessen the urge to drink. She found a physician who prescribed it, and she followed the basic elements of the method on her own. It worked insofar as she drank less when she took it, but it made her feel terrible for days after.

That's when her frustration led her to me. We started by taking a long history of her life, her drinking, and her attempts to change up to that point. I explained that there were various techniques for using naltrexone effectively and we talked about experimenting until we found what worked. But I also told Julia she'd need to be ready for what was likely to come. Once we got her drinking under control (and we would), some real discomfort would start peeking through. I told her that this is where the real work lies—understanding the discomfort, exploring it, and fixing it. Julia listened, but sort of shrugged me off.

"Sure," she said. "Let's take care of the drinking."

It wasn't hard to see that deep inside, she felt everything would be solved if she could just take care of her alcohol problem.

Julia's Way Back Out—The "End" Is the Beginning

Without too much difficulty, Julia was able to find a dosage and medication schedule that, along with careful planning of her drinking days, resulted in no overdrinking and no terrible medication side effects. But she was worried. She had planned a trip to visit a friend who had always been a heavy drinking partner, and she had no idea how she would handle it. Julia was afraid she'd go along with the heavy alcohol consumption and reverse all of her progress.

Finally, we were getting to the real work! This was exactly the sort of negative belief and self-talk we wanted to root out.

I asked Julia, "What other area of your life requires that you are always perfect in order to be able to progress forward?"

Julia couldn't come up with a satisfactory example.

"See," I said, "you need to take the pressure off of yourself. This constant striving for perfection is what will bring you down, not a night of heavy drinking."

It took us nearly the entire hour, but Julia began to see the progress she'd made and realize that she didn't have to discount it. But we had more work to do.

In our next session I took Julia through a visualization exercise. In all of her previous attempts, Julia never truly allowed herself to think of an "ideal" outcome for her life without alcohol or with "normal," occasional use. I had Julia close her eyes and work through a mental movie of what she hoped her first evening with her friend would look like. How would she tell her friend she was hoping to drink less (or not drink at all)? How would the evening progress? What would they do together?

In the past, Julia left all these elements to chance, but those days were gone. As with all my clients, it took a while for Julia to come up with this scenario. It made her uncomfortable, and I had to step back and explain that if we don't *actively* change our learned patterns, our brains will continue to play them out as in the past. In the case of her visit with her friend, her brain knew exactly how to drink at this friend's house—excessively!

Julia had to practice a different behavior. But by visualizing and working though her ideal scenario, her brain now had something specific to grasp. She was creating a new pattern that was more desirable than the heavy drinking one.

Whether she would be able to stick to this new version of the visit wasn't clear yet, but at least Julia had a new story to fall back on if the old story began to play out.

Julia's trip didn't go perfectly. She didn't drink anywhere near the quantity of alcohol she'd consumed on previous visits, but she drank more frequently than she wanted to, and she didn't take the naltrexone every time she drank. She was dismayed and frustrated.

When she got back, we spent two sessions working out what went wrong and what she could have improved on. I made sure to repeat the question she regularly needed to ask to herself: "If you look at your drinking over this past week versus your drinking before we started working together, how do you feel you're doing?"

Julia told me that she felt she was doing better, but she felt guilty for not meeting her mark. I made sure she knew that I understood, but I reminded her that this was her first real attempt at behavioral change, and it had worked. She drank less with her friend than she ever had before. If she could repeat that experience over time, she would gradually create bigger and bigger change. Now Julia was truly on board!

The Present Reality—Practicing Recovery

We repeated these sorts of sessions for two months. Julia made constant progress with limiting her drinking, and she was excited to discover that she had more energy. But she was really surprised to find out how many parts of her life she had been hiding from with her drinking. All kinds of fears and disappointments reared their heads. She worried she wasn't worthy of all of her success. She feared that the biggest project she'd ever taken on would fail terribly. She experienced the full brunt of her dissatisfaction with her health and weight gain, and she acknowledged her belief that her social circle would disappear if she didn't drink with them as she always had. Bit by bit, we worked on ways for her to create new images for the new life she was creating. It was deliberate, purposeful, and much faster than she had imagined.

Julia and I kept in touch for months after our initial work together, and she continued to practice using her new tools and strategies. About two months after our last session, I received a wonderful message from her saying that she "no longer felt as if alcohol was a significant part of her life." She told me:

"I feel more clearheaded every morning and more enthusiastic about my day. I feel much more confident and much more able to communicate my message to the world, which was my ultimate goal in the first place."

Julia drinks, occasionally, and she successfully uses her tools when she does. But her most important outcome and biggest victory is that she finally feels "normal" again for the first time in decades. She is making ongoing, incremental changes to improve her life now that changes around using alcohol are successfully behind her. (You can find more about her experience at www.igntdrecovery.com.)

The IGNTD Principles

With IGNTD Recovery, old assumptions are questioned, opening up a whole new world of possibilities. If your experience is anything like that of the hundreds of people I've seen over the years, the possibility of such an approach excites you and makes you hopeful that you too can find a way out of the mess and into a life you're proud of.

To be clear, this "shame-free, judgment-free, rules-free" approach doesn't mean "work-free." You'll have go through the work in order to get to the other side, but the process delivers results all along the way. The approach generates hope rather than creating familiar feelings of dread and emptiness.

> *To be clear, this "shame-free, judgment-free, rules-free" approach doesn't mean "work-free."*

The method stands on three principles that will serve as guardrails for the rest of your life:

1. Honest Exploration

2. Radical Acceptance

3. Individualized Transformation

You will finally get honest about your life, and you'll use the skill of honest exploration whenever you need to adjust or right things when something starts going wrong.

You'll begin to see and accept exactly where you are at any given moment—what the Buddha taught about seeing the truth without being attached to it.

And you'll develop, refine, and continually revisit the tools and practices that give you the life you want. No one is static—the roles and identities we have today will continue to evolve.

Honest Exploration

Many people who turn to me for help are looking in the wrong place. They've been told their addictive behavior is the problem for so long that they themselves have forgotten the underlying reasons for their problem.

Those who struggle with alcohol and drugs are told they are lying about their addiction, and they feel like "liars" because of all the pain, shame, confusion, and trauma they have hidden from themselves and others for so long.

Honest exploration involves looking into the life experiences that have brought you to this point, because you can't address what you are not aware of. Done in a judgment-free, supportive manner, this exploration can uncover damaging beliefs, unhelpful thought patterns or habits, and unrealistic expectations. For so many of the people I work with, this process takes time, but once completed it forever changes their perception of the actual struggle.

Once you understand your past, it's important to understand exactly what you are currently struggling with. Using the same nonjudgmental approach, you'll explore the biological, psychological, environmental, and spiritual (if appropriate) aspects of your struggle. If there are multiple aspects to your condition, you have to identify the specific balance that is relevant to you.

So what if everyone out there says all addicts are the same? You've known the nuances of the issues you've been struggling with along the way. You know the complexity of the life that has led you here, as well as the things you've hidden from others.

This awareness will immediately remove the mystery around your struggles. And if there's one thing I've found to be true, it's that we are most afraid of the things we don't understand. You have to get to a place where you truly and honestly understand what's made you who you are.

Since I believe you cannot accomplish something you don't believe is possible, understanding your own limiting beliefs and thought patterns is a crucial part of honest exploration. If you don't believe in the task you're embarking on, then confirmation bias will continue to make sure you focus on the evidence that you're failing. If you continue seeing yourself as a failure, you will convey that to others, making everyone around you believe you are doomed. This has to be changed.

The constant barrage of messages from society that addiction is a permanent state damages your own belief in yourself and your ability to beat this addiction problem. But it's not true. It's not what research tells us, and it's not what I've seen happen hundreds of time.

That's why, after identifying unhelpful beliefs, thoughts, and habits, you'll break them down and replace them with new beliefs that support where you want to go.

The good news is that you've already started doing this by simply getting to this point in the book.

Radical Acceptance

The process of shifting your beliefs and understanding who you are leads you to a new, eyes-wide-open view of yourself, your community, and your role in the world. You will undoubtedly uncover aspects of your past and present that you are unhappy with—past trauma you've looked away from, personality characteristics you wish you didn't have, and aspects of your life you've neglected for so long they've become embarrassing. Still, if you truly want to get to a better place, it means coming to terms with each and every one of these revelations.

It can be tempting to judge the aspects of yourself that you're unhappy with, but that judgment leads nowhere useful. Complete acceptance of the specifics of your struggle allows you to continually move forward with a clear mind and a level of motivation that simply will not be undermined.

I tell many of my clients a story to explain this approach to assessment and radical acceptance. I stand 5'10" on my tiptoes. I love playing basketball, but I can't dunk to save my life. This fact surprises no one, but it also has the distinction of being true. Since I like playing basketball, I could feel terrible about my inability to jump high enough to dunk the ball. I mean, even Spud Web, a retired NBA point guard (who is substantially shorter than me at 5'7"), can dunk! But feeling ashamed and embarrassed about this will do nothing to help me dunk.

I have two clear choices: 1) I can accept it and move on, playing without the joy of dunking, or 2) I can accept it and do the hard work necessary to jump higher, which will include hours and hours at the gym strengthening my legs and practicing jumping incrementally higher until I reach my goal. With enough work and the right training tools, there's a chance I might get there. But regardless of which path I choose, the first step is to accept reality. Otherwise I will be both unable to meet my goal and feeling less than for it—a lose-lose proposition.

To make matters worse, being unable to accept your circumstances has been a primary reason for your addictive behavior. I remember the internal dialogues well:

"People don't like me" becomes "Let's get drunk."

"I can't study" turns to a dependence on amphetamines.

Terry didn't like her marriage, but instead of accepting that reality and working on it, she drank more alcohol. Avoiding our problems will only make them worse, and my 5'10" frame isn't going to ever dunk a basketball if all I do is pretend that I can.

Julia avoided her feelings of inadequacy, Terry avoided her relationship problems and discontent with her circumstances, and I avoided my constant inability to make my parents proud and feel okay about my own insecurities and inadequacies.

Honest exploration shines a light on our previously dark path. Radical honesty allows us to walk along it to move forward.

Individualized Transformation

The third foundational principle of IGNTD Recovery is all about hope, individual goals, and the true purpose of your recovery. It provides clarity about who you are and where you are in your life and recovery. I can almost guarantee that your true motivations have very little to do with substance use.

Don't misunderstand this point. Stopping or reducing your substance use may be *very* important to achieving your goals. But you need to know what you're trying to achieve in life so you can get there. With that clarity, you can find the support and techniques you need to get you there.

Everyone needs tools. Carpenters use a whole set of hammers and screwdrivers, drills and levels to build a house; mechanics rely on bolts and wrenches, lifts and meters to fix engines and motors. You are going to need the tools most relevant to you, which depends on the specific circumstances and the factors you've uncovered and accepted previously.

The tools of recovery may include biological interventions (medications) or physiological treatments such as biofeedback. They may involve psychological treatment with a professional therapist and possibly behavioral exercises for you to practice on your own. They will very likely involve tools for ongoing exploration and self-knowledge so you never again find yourself in a position of unawareness. The tools you learn will become your new compass and protection. They will support you as you construct a healthier set of habits while changing the way you see yourself, relate to the world, and plan for success. They will also include steps to create more openness and intimacy with your "tribe."

Many people want to do this work alone. They are ashamed of the pain they've caused others and the destruction they've brought on. In the process, they make themselves their own judge and jury, which does not help them get better.

Many people want to do this work alone. They are ashamed of the pain they've caused others and the destruction they've brought on. In the process, they make themselves their own judge and jury, which does not help them get better.

By the time I actually managed to stay sober for a while, I had tried to stop using meth so many times that I'd lost count. I would wake up in the morning feeling pretty damn good, and I'd tell myself, "You don't need to use today." But by 3:00 p.m., I'd have loaded up my pipe and started smoking again. It was so demoralizing. I couldn't admit it to anyone else because I felt like a failure.

You've probably felt it before too—the numbing sorrow of having "failed" once more after trying to quit. You may be thinking to yourself, "If I do the work of honest exploration and radical acceptance, I should be able to handle the tools and steps for transformation on my own as well."

Having help is an incredibly important component of almost any worthwhile transformation. Think of any other really important or big things you've done in your life and identify those that required help versus those you could do completely alone. Coaches, teachers, parents, friends, and colleagues have been there for you throughout your life (and if they haven't, then I already know the struggles you've experienced and the areas we'll need to work on) and you'll want them there again for this. We'll talk about this more in the nine steps that follow, but stay open to getting the help you need and using the principles of IGNTD to set you on a new course.

The Nine Steps of IGNTD Recovery

Putting IGNTD Recovery into action in your own life means living the foundational principles of exploration, acceptance, and transformation. Those three concepts are your guardrails. Are you continually learning, opening your mind and emotions? Are you accepting where you are, what's happening in your life, what you're feeling, doing, and contributing? Are you continuing to evolve, grow, and deal with new challenges, setbacks, and aspirations in work, love, community, and a meaningful life?

To put these foundations in place, here are the specific IGNTD Recovery steps we will follow:

1. Expand your understanding of addiction and recovery.

2. Uncover your formative experiences.

3. Address and challenge your underlying beliefs.

4. Examine your current struggles.

5. Release your shame.

6. Redefine and crystallize your goals.

7. Build and customize your personal recovery tool kit.

8. Find your tribe and create accountability.

9. Continue to refine and implement the foundations and steps of IGNTD Recovery.

Step 1. Expand your understanding of addiction and recovery.

Cementing the process that you've started by reading this book, we must begin by intellectually understanding—and gradually accepting—the idea that addiction is not one thing for all people. The causes, outcomes, and journeys are unique for each individual. We must create a safe starting point for exploration, understanding that our chances of success are greatly dependent on our own belief in the potential for true addiction recovery.

This step allows you to open up to outcomes and tools that may have seemed irrelevant or inappropriate to you before. When you expand the concept of what your "addiction" struggle means, you become more flexible in your adoption of recovery. This is the step that took me the longest and is one of the reasons behind my desire to give you a shortcut to happiness. This is the step that allowed Terry to decide to take a long break from drinking; it's the step that led John to finally believe there was hope. It's also the type of thinking that has allowed countless of my clients to choose lifelong abstinence because they wanted it.

To begin Step 1:

- Get explicit about your current beliefs about "addicts" and "alcoholics" and identify the ones that you find most limiting.

Step 2. Uncover your formative experiences.

With the groundwork laid, we can begin exploring the experiences that have formed our current beliefs about ourselves, about others, and about the process of getting help. We take on this exploration with a constant eye toward any judgment, shame, and discomfort that might arise, recognizing that these are all intertwined and ripe for further exploration. This step can take some time, as it delves into long-hidden crevices of your very being.

This is where Julia uncovered her unhealthy family relationships. It's where John discovered that his distant parents created a framework for intimate relationships that left him feeling alone, even when he was married. This step allowed me to understand that my early perceptions of failure in school drove my apparent lack of motivation for decades and started me on my downward spiral.

To begin Step 2:

- Complete or review all the exercises at the end of each chapter, especially Chapters 2, 3, and 4.

Step 3. Address and challenge you underlying beliefs.

After exploring your experiences and gaining a better understanding of your underlying beliefs about yourself, we begin a process of changing our story about who we are, our worth, and our potential. We may have thought of ourselves as lazy, dumb, or unmotivated. We may have seen ourselves as being unlovable or incapable of loving. Understanding the sources of these unhelpful and often irrational beliefs is important, but often it is not enough to release their hold on us. This step addresses our past experiences and focuses on actively changing our beliefs in order to adopt new beliefs and allow for growth.

In this step, Julia discovered that she is no longer the hapless little girl whose efforts to be the best started as a child when she had to cope with her brothers' aggression. It was in this step that Terry realized she could challenge her belief that she was stuck in a life she hated and was unable to change.

To begin Step 3:

- Name one explicit negative belief about yourself and identify at least one or two situations in your life that suggest this belief might be false.

Step 4. Examine your current struggles.

With a clearer understanding and acceptance of the path we've taken to our present circumstances, we conduct a thorough assessment of our current struggles, making sure to examine not only our addictive use (and behaviors) but also the surrounding factors. We begin looking at our overall quality of life in the present moment, all the while trying to minimize judgment of self and overwhelm with the impact we're having on others.

While it isn't always comfortable to take an objective hard look at ourselves, this is work that allows you to understand what needs to be done. Julia, undertaking a full assessment, began seeing the role of health and intimacy in her drinking. My own self-assessment revealed long-standing impulsivity and attention problems that I needed to address head on.

To begin Step 4:

* Separate yourself from the problem of drinking, identify an area of your life that you've been neglecting, and rate your level of satisfaction with it (for example: relationships, children, health, finances, career, purpose, spirituality, exercise, fun).

Step 5. Release shame.

Having come to a clear understanding of your path to the present and the specific factors involved in your current struggles, it's time to really work on radical acceptance of where you are.

You've surely uncovered things that make you uncomfortable and beliefs you wish you didn't hold. To the best of your ability, and understanding that the process of releasing shame is ongoing, you sincerely accept that you have done your very best to this point and that your future work will be taken on best without the weight of shame and self-doubt.

This process is not simple because, for many of us, shame has been pervasive and many of the labels that have been placed upon us are universally looked down upon. However, in order to move forward to the next step, we have to accept our reality.

It took me years to get through this step, and I am constantly continuing to work on it. When John realized that his struggles didn't have to continue and his inability to connect with his wife was not his fault, but rather a product of a multitude of factors in his past, it allowed him to move forward with a firm motivation to continue. He was able to have new conversations with his wife, and she felt more open to the idea that change was possible.

This is where you figure out that the opposite of success isn't failure—it's giving up.

To begin Step 5:

* Write down the specific ways shame has held you back in life and kept you from moving forward with important areas of your life.

Step 6. Redefine and crystallize your goals.

Understanding your path to "now," and coming to terms with it, you are ready to do the work of clarifying where you are trying to go. Before, you thought you'd define success by simply avoiding the problem behavior. But now you see that it's much bigger than that. You move from what you don't want to want you *do* want. It's a switch from what I call the "small version" of ourselves to a more open and bigger one. Clients say things like:

"I want to stop fighting with friends when I'm drunk" to *"I want to get along better with my wife."*

"I want to stop using and driving so irresponsibly" to *"I want to go more places and do more things with friends and in the community- I want to be in a place where I can give back"*

"I want to stop feeling like my whole life is a trigger from the moment I wake up and just try to get through the day" to *"I want to finally pursue my college degree."*

When we look at our specific expectations for success and develop clear motivations for succeeding, we can actually measure our results and define steps and time frames for their achievement. Like a well-prepared traveler, we now find ourselves armed with a recovery map that consists of our origin *and* our destination. I love this step in the process because so many clients find themselves choosing goals they never could have imagined.

With an eye toward real happiness, this is where Terry chose to abstain and where Julia found herself drinking substantially less than she had originally intended to. I make revisiting goals and setting new ones an annual process in my life.

To begin Step 6:

* If you could have success with your addiction, what would that look like? Fully visualize and write down or record that story.

Step 7. Build and customize your personal recovery tool kit.

In order to increase the chances of a successful recovery journey, you'll learn, practice, refine, and master your own personal tool kit of techniques, processes, habits, and reflections. You attend to your individual needs by paying special attention to tools that have been shown to be specifically useful for the sort of gaps you've uncovered in your earlier self-assessment and beliefs work.

Different tools work for different people. Terry received the most benefit from cognitive behavioral work and meditation. Julia loved the effect her medication gave her while incorporating heavy doses of cognitive restructuring work. I rely on exercise, purposeful work, and short mindfulness practices to continue moving me in the right direction. What will your tool kit consist of?

To begin Step 7:

* Commit to exploring therapy, medication, self-help meetings, or the IGNTD Recovery online course to gain concrete tools for your journey.

Step 8. Find your tribe and create accountability.

The transformation you are undertaking is wholesale. It encompasses every aspect of who you are, how you see yourself, and how others see you. Through the shame-releasing work you've done, you have let go of some of the social anxiety and fear that has held you back. But many of us continue to avoid intimate connections with others by distancing ourselves either physically or emotionally. We've hurt and disappointed a lot of people, and we stopped trusting ourselves a long time ago, and this puts a barrier between us and anyone else we may hurt.

You'll have to beat down the shame that makes it especially hard to identify, and then reach out to, the people who will be most effects as your support (as well as those who are currently most damaging to your efforts). As you release your shame, your social fears will also diminish, and you'll begin to see how the support of others, rather than their approval, can be a powerful tool in your recovery journey.

Identifying the relationships that best fit your purpose and the work you must do to create real intimacy with those close to you will go a long way toward creating a strong and lasting foundation for your continued success. You'll practice figuring out how to be honest with people throughout the process so they can be there for you. The more open and trusting you become, the more open and trusting others become toward you. The feeling of communion you will get from finding a true support network is impossible to overvalue.

Who could have imagined that the people I ran from the most—my parents and my closest friends—would become the people I share my struggles with first now? Julia and John could have never imagined having the forthright and honest conversations they now regularly have with their spouses. Everything is easier when you know who to rely on and how to feel safe.

If you have *not* benefited from a trusted relationship with someone who could support your recovery, use this step to ask yourself if some outside perspective, skill, support, and accountability would help you move your life and recovery to a whole new level. Now that you have the insight of IGNTD Recovery, you will be on firmer ground to get support that will be truly helpful.

To begin Step 8:

* Identify the single most likely person that you could rely on for shame-free support.

Step 9. Continue to refine and implement the foundations and steps of IGNTD Recovery.

As you go through these steps and see your life and relationships shifting (especially with the reference point of where you've been), you begin to build awareness that you will continue to learn and change. Continual self-assessment and exploration paired with shame-free revisions of your needs and goals allow you to refine the path you take. Practicing humility, examining your gaps, and being mindful of your opportunities for growth through honest interactions with your support network will ensure that you continue righting yourself, even in the face of challenging circumstances.

My work is never done, and my self-discovery is ongoing. The beautiful thing about this process is that each new discovery opens up entirely new opportunities to make life better. Now doing the work produces joy rather than pain.

Obviously, Step 9 is a sort of coda, directing you to go back to the beginning to keep exploring on a continuous basis. This isn't meant as an indication that something is wrong with you—it's a reality. You change, your world changes, and your needs change. Life is an ongoing learning opportunity.

To begin Step 9:

* Record where you are right this moment with your problems and goals, as well as any changes and progress you've made, so you have a reference point as you progress. Recognize the need for ongoing refinement and improvement in any worthwhile skill or habit.

The Process of IGNTD Recovery

The IGNTD Recovery process creates transformation, but it does so in a way that is considerate of each person's unique needs and circumstances without shirking their personal responsibility for change. Each of these steps encompasses many techniques, skills, and supports—but you can begin at the simplest level to work through the ideas, spending time every day thinking, writing, observing, experimenting, and sharing (when you're ready). Small insights and steps accumulate to make big changes, and perfection should never be a requirement.

Outside help can be useful—even essential—along the way, especially when it comes to important physiological issues such as withdrawal, detoxification, and medications. But you need to believe in your ability to change in order to increase the odds that support and expert help will produce actual results in your life.

Step 1 expands your understanding of addiction, which allows you to believe in your ability to succeed again.

Steps 2, 3, and 4 allow you to understand and accept yourself as you are, putting aside the belief that you are "damaged."

Step 5 means directly coming to terms with and working through the shame that comes with addiction so you can accept your past and present as parts of the journey that brought you here. This step is about recovering your self-respect and self-efficacy, as well as shedding the negative self-image that has kept you isolated and hopeless.

Step 6 is all about creating a deeper and bigger vision for where you want to go. It's being excited about the journey you are undertaking while removing the fear you've had that life in recovery will be meaningless and joyless. By having goals you're excited about, you'll be able to imagine what success looks like and have real, measurable ways to know when you've gotten there.

Step 7 provides you with practical tools to make the trek from your current starting point to your desired goal. Armed with your tool kit, you'll be prepared for oncoming challenges, which will reduce your anxieties and assure you that you're prepared for success.

Step 8 focuses on intentionally building a community that allows you to transcend your addiction struggles. It focuses on achieving your greater purpose and goals in communion with people who truly care for you, the real you that you are working so hard to cultivate.

Finally, Step 9 reminds you that you need to consciously live the principles of exploration, acceptance, and individual transformation as your life, struggles, and aspirations continue to evolve.

The feeling of putting your "addiction" struggles behind you and taking on the journey of recovery and self-improvement creates pride and joy where shame and dread once prospered. As you continue traveling this path, you will one day look back and see your current struggles as a powerful memory—a hero's journey of your own.

That's when you'll know you are ignited.

Taking on the journey of recovery and self-improvement creates pride and joy where shame and dread once prospered.

EXERCISE: *Simple Steps to Start Your Recovery*

Now that you've completed the reading of this introduction to the IGNTD Recovery model, some elements most likely speak directly to your experience, struggles, hopes, and fears. Following the IGNTD Recovery principles and steps set out in this chapter, this exercise will give you a start in applying the framework:

1. Which of the three principles or nine steps speak most directly and immediately to your:

    a. biggest addiction struggles?

    b. strongest hopes for recovery?

    c. most debilitating fears?

2. For each of your three answers in Question 1, what have you learned through the reading of this book that empowers you to create change around each of those areas? Be specific in writing down one, two, or three specific actions or beliefs you can use to address that change.

3. If you had to identify your biggest current source of shame, what would it be?

4. Revisiting our earlier exercise at the close of Chapter 1, what is the number one reason it is important for you to make now the time for real change in your addiction?

5. Are there one or two actions you can commit to for the next day or week? It can be as small or big a commitment as you're comfortable

with. (In my experience, the fact that you are giving yourself space to think again—and differently—about your problem gives you the element of hope, which makes all the difference.)

Afterword

wrote this book in order to provide some measure of help to the millions of people who are struggling without any sense of hope. I believe there is a path for everyone to move past the suffering that alcohol, drug, and other addictions can bring, and it largely hinges on the need to bring back a measure of choice and control for those who need help.

By picking up this book, you have already committed to change, and wherever that change may take you, I applaud your efforts. I know the feeling of despair, and I recognize the fear of paving your own path toward a better life. I hope this book has provided what I intended: hope and direction toward your ultimate success.

Good luck on your journey and writing your new story. I hope to see you at IGNTD.com/Recovery, on Facebook, and at events, workshops, our free online webinars, and our inspiring online programs. If I can be part of your recovery family and tribe, I'm there for you.

Acknowledgments

While there are too many names to mention, I want to specifically acknowledge the work of Alan Marlatt, Stanton Peele, Andrew Tatarsky, Dee-Dee Stout, Tom Horvath, Thomas McLellan, and my graduate advisors, David Jentsh and Peter Bentler, as well as my previous partner Marc Kern.

I also want to thank those of you who read or worked on early versions of the manuscript in order to help direct the effort—Alex, Julia, Matthew, and my dear father-in-law, Reuben.

Thank you, Janet—without your help, this manuscript would have never taken the shape it finally did. Thanks for helping me pick and chisel this thing into existence.

To everyone else who has been part of my journey, including the staff at the rehab I attended and the couples that help Sophie and me make sure our relationship stands strong—thank you for being in my life.

Notes

1. Key Substance Use and Mental Health Indicators in the United States: Results from the 2016 National Survey on Drug Use and Health. In: Center for Behavioral Health Statistics and Quality, ed. Vol HHS Publication No. SMA 17-5044, NSDUH Series H-52: Substance Abuse and Mental Health Services Administration; 2017.

2. Jaffe A, Murphy D, Shaheed T, Coleman A, Hser Y. Not ashamed anymore: Longitudinal changes in barriers to treatment entry for online treatment seekers. *Drug & Alcohol Dependence.*140:e95.

3. Ward MM, Ullrich F, Matthews K, et al. Who Does Not Receive Treatment for Cancer? *Journal of Oncology Practice.* 2013;9(1):20-26.

4. Rudd RA, Aleshire N, Zibbell JE, Matthew Gladden R. Increases in drug and opioid overdose deaths—United States, 2000–2014. *American Journal of Transplantation.* 2016;16(4):1323-1327.

5. Stahre M, Roeber J, Kanny D, Brewer RD, Zhang X. Contribution of Excessive Alcohol Consumption to Deaths and Years of Potential Life Lost in the United States. *Preventing Chronic Disease.* 2014;11:E109.

6. Rudd RA. Increases in drug and opioid-involved overdose deaths— United States, 2010–2015. *MMWR Morbidity and mortality weekly report.* 2016;65.

7. Synder HN, Statistics BoJ, Justice UDo, Programs OoJ. Arrest in the United States, 1990–2010. *Washington, DC: US Department of Justice, Office of Justice Programs, Bureau of Justice Statistics.* 2012.

8. Nadelmann EA. Drug prohibition in the United States: Costs, consequences, and alternatives. *Science.* 1989;245(4921):939-947.

9. McLellan AT, Lewis DC, O'Brien CP, Kleber HD. Drug dependence, a chronic medical illness: Implications for treatment, insurance, and outcomes evaluation. *Journal of the American Medical Association.* 2000;284(13):1689-1695.

10. Stoltzfus KM. Spiritual Interventions in Substance Abuse Treatment and Prevention. *Journal of Religion & Spirituality in Social Work: Social Thought.* 2007;26(4):49-69.

11. Murray TS, Malcarne VL, Goggin K. Alcohol-related God/higher power control beliefs, locus of control, and recovery within the Alcoholics Anonymous paradigm. *Alcoholism Treatment Quarterly.* 2003;21(3):23-39.

12. Stone D. Exactly How Many Times Does the Big Book Mention God? 2016; https://bigbookwizardry.wordpress.com/2016/02/11/exactly-how-many-times-does-the-big-book-mention-god/.

13. Kendler KS, Liu X-Q, Gardner CO, McCullough ME, Larson D, Prescott CA. Dimensions of Religiosity and Their Relationship to Lifetime Psychiatric and Substance Use Disorders. *American Journal of Psychiatry.* 2003;160(3):496-503.

14. Wills TA, Yaeger AM, Sandy JM. Buffering effect of religiosity for adolescent substance use. *Psychology of Addictive Behaviors.* 2003;17(1):24-31.

15. Li EC, Feifer C, Strohm M. A pilot study: Locus of control and spiritual beliefs in alcoholics anonymous and smart recovery members. *Addictive Behaviors.* 2000;25(4):633-640.

16. Rohsenow DJ, O'Leary MR. Locus of Control Research on Alcoholic Populations: A Review. I. Development, Scales, and Treatment. *International Journal of the Addictions.* 1978;13(1):55-78.

17. Khantzian EJ. The Self-Medication Hypothesis of Substance Use Disorders: A Reconsideration and Recent Applications. *Harvard Review of Psychiatry.* 1997;4(5):231-244.

18. Kessler RC, Nelson CB, McGonagle KA, Edlund MJ, Frank RG, Leaf PJ. The epidemiology of co-occurring addictive and mental disorders: implications for prevention and service utilization. *American Journal of Orthopsychiatry.* 1996;66(1):17.

19. Brady KT, Sinha R. Co-occurring mental and substance use disorders: the neurobiological effects of chronic stress. *American Journal of Psychiatry.* 2005;162(8):1483-1493.

20. Kilpatrick DG, Ruggiero KJ, Acierno R, Saunders BE, Resnick HS, Best CL. Violence and risk of PTSD, major depression, substance abuse/dependence, and comorbidity: results from the National Survey of Adolescents. *Journal of consulting and clinical psychology.* 2003;71(4):692.

21. Molnar BE, Buka SL, Kessler RC. Child sexual abuse and subsequent psychopathology: results from the National Comorbidity Survey. *American journal of public health.* 2001;91(5):753.

22. Kilpatrick DG, Saunders BE, Smith DW. Youth victimization: Prevalence and implications. Research in brief. *Washington, DC: US Department of Justice, Office of Justice Programs.* 2003.

23. Hien DA, Wells EA, Jiang H, et al. Multi-site randomized trial of behavioral interventions for women with co-occurring PTSD and substance use disorders. *Journal of consulting and clinical psychology.* 2009;77(4):607-619.

24. Holdeman TC. Invisible wounds of war: Psychological and cognitive injuries, their consequences, and services to assist recovery. *Psychiatric Services.* 2009;60(2):273-273.

25. Leshner AI. Addiction Is a Brain Disease, and It Matters. *Science.* 1997;278(5335):45-47.

26. Kendler KS, Neale MC, Kessler RC, Heath AC, Eaves LJ. Major depression and generalized anxiety disorder: Same genes, (partly) different environments? *Archives of General Psychiatry.* 1992;49(9):716-722.

27. Shih RA, Belmonte PL, Zandi PP. A review of the evidence from family, twin and adoption studies for a genetic contribution to adult psychiatric disorders. *International Review of Psychiatry.* 2004;16(4):260-283.

28. Kendler KS, Prescott CA, Myers J, Neale MC. The structure of genetic and environmental risk factors for common psychiatric and substance use disorders in men and women. *Archives of General Psychiatry.* 2003;60(9):929-937.

29. Caspi A, Sugden K, Moffitt TE, et al. Influence of life stress on depression: moderation by a polymorphism in the 5-HTT gene. *Science.* 2003;301(5631):386-389.

30. Caspi A, Moffitt TE. Gene–environment interactions in psychiatry: joining forces with neuroscience. *Nature Reviews Neuroscience.* 2006;7(7):583.

31. Hyman SE, Malenka RC, Nestler EJ. Neural mechanisms of addiction: the role of reward-related learning and memory. *Annu Rev Neurosci.* 2006;29:565-598.

32. Nestler EJ, Barrot M, Self DW. ΔFosB: A sustained molecular switch for addiction. *Proceedings of the National Academy of Sciences.* 2001;98(20):11042-11046.

33. Robins LN, Helzer JE, Hesselbrock M, Wish E. Vietnam veterans three years after Vietnam: How our study changed our view of heroin. *The American Journal on Addictions.* 2010;19(3):203-211.

34. Dawson DA, Grant BF, Stinson FS, Chou PS, Huang B, Ruan W. Recovery from DSM-IV alcohol dependence: United States, 2001–2002. *Addiction.* 2005;100(3):281-292.

35. Jaffe A. Two Forms of Alcoholism. 2010; https://www.psychologytoday. com/blog/all-about-addiction/201008/two-forms-alcoholism.

36. Di Chiara G, Imperato A. Drugs abused by humans preferentially increase synaptic dopamine concentrations in the mesolimbic system of freely moving rats. *Proceedings of the National Academy of Sciences.* 1988;85(14):5274-5278.

37. Yokel RA, Wise RA. Attenuation of intravenous amphetamine reinforcement by central dopamine blockade in rats. *Psychopharmacology.* 1976;48(3):311-318.

38. Pettit HO, Ettenberg A, Bloom FE, Koob GF. Destruction of dopamine in the nucleus accumbens selectively attenuates cocaine but not heroin self-administration in rats. *Psychopharmacology.* 1984;84(2):167-173.

39. Haney M, Ramesh D, Glass A, Pavlicova M, Bedi G, Cooper ZD. Naltrexone maintenance decreases cannabis self-administration and subjective effects in daily cannabis smokers. *Neuropsychopharmacology.* 2015;40(11):2489.

40. Savage SR, Kirsh KL, Passik SD. Challenges in Using Opioids to Treat Pain in Persons With Substance Use Disorders. *Addiction Science & Clinical Practice.* 2008;4(2):4-25.

41. Nestler EJ. Molecular basis of long-term plasticity underlying addiction. *Nature reviews neuroscience.* 2001;2(2):119.

42. Koob GF, Le Moal M. Drug abuse: hedonic homeostatic dysregulation. *Science.* 1997;278(5335):52-58.

43. Center for Substance Abuse Treatment. Medication-assisted treatment for opioid addiction in opioid treatment programs. 2005.

44. Mayo-Smith MF. Pharmacological management of alcohol withdrawal: a meta-analysis and evidence-based practice guideline. *Jama.* 1997;278(2):144-151.

45. Baldwin DS, Anderson IM, Nutt DJ, et al. Evidence-based guidelines for the pharmacological treatment of anxiety disorders: recommendations from the British Association for Psychopharmacology. *Journal of Psychopharmacology.* 2005;19(6):567-596.

46. Scott WC, Kaiser D, Othmer S, Sideroff SI. Effects of an EEG biofeedback protocol on a mixed substance abusing population. *The American journal of drug and alcohol abuse.* 2005;31(3):455-469.

47. Seidler GH, Wagner FE. Comparing the efficacy of EMDR and trauma-focused cognitive-behavioral therapy in the treatment of PTSD: a meta-analytic study. *Psychological medicine.* 2006;36(11):1515-1522.

48. Kosten TR, Domingo CB, Shorter D, et al. Vaccine for cocaine dependence: a randomized double-blind placebo-controlled efficacy trial. *Drug & Alcohol Dependence.* 2014;140:42-47.

49. Goldstein RZ, Volkow ND. Drug addiction and its underlying neurobiological basis: neuroimaging evidence for the involvement of the frontal cortex. *American Journal of Psychiatry.* 2002;159(10):1642-1652.

50. Volkow ND, Wang G-J, Telang F, et al. Cocaine cues and dopamine in dorsal striatum: mechanism of craving in cocaine addiction. *Journal of Neuroscience.* 2006;26(24):6583-6588.

51. Jaffe A, Pham J, Tarash I, Getty SS, Fanselow MS, Jentsch JD. The Absence of Blocking Innicotine High-Responders as a Possible Factor in the Development of Nicotine Dependence? *The Open Addiction Journal.* 2014;7(1).

52. Winstanley CA, Olausson P, Taylor JR, Jentsch JD. Insight into the relationship between impulsivity and substance abuse from studies using animal models. *Alcoholism: Clinical and Experimental Research.* 2010;34(8):1306-1318.

53. Kreek MJ, Nielsen DA, Butelman ER, LaForge KS. Genetic influences on impulsivity, risk taking, stress responsivity and vulnerability to drug abuse and addiction. *Nature neuroscience.* 2005;8(11):1450.

54. Kendler KS, Myers J, Prescott CA. Specificity of genetic and environmental risk factors for symptoms of cannabis, cocaine, alcohol, caffeine, and nicotine dependence. *Archives of General Psychiatry.* 2007;64(11):1313-1320.

55. Goldman D, Oroszi G, Ducci F. The genetics of addictions: uncovering the genes. *Nature Reviews Genetics.* 2005;6(7):521.

56. Van den Bree MB, Johnson EO, Neale MC, Pickens RW. Genetic and environmental influences on drug use and abuse/dependence in male and female twins. *Drug & Alcohol Dependence.* 1998;52(3):231-241.

57. Peele S, Brodsky A. Addiction is a social disease. 1976.

58. Alexander B. *The globalization of addiction: A study in poverty of the spirit.* Oxford University Press; 2010.

59. Centers for Disease Control and Prevention. Vital signs: binge drinking prevalence, frequency, and intensity among adults-United States, 2010. *MMWR Morbidity and mortality weekly report.* 2012;61(1):14.

60. Cashin JR, Presley CA, Meilman PW. Alcohol use in the Greek system: Follow the leader? *Journal of Studies on Alcohol.* 1998;59(1):63-70.

61. Wechsler H, Dowdall G, Moeykens M. of Binge Drinking in College. *Jama.* 1994;272:1672-1677.

62. Dielman TE, Campanelli PC, Shope JT, Butchart AT. Susceptibility to peer pressure, self-esteem, and health locus of control as correlates of adolescent substance abuse. *Health education quarterly.* 1987;14(2):207-221.

63. Lender ME, Martin JK. *Drinking in America: A history.* Simon and Schuster; 1987.

64. US Department of Health and Human Service *Dietary Guidelines for Americans 2015-2020.* Skyhorse Publishing Inc.; 2017.

65. Baumrind D. The influence of parenting style on adolescent competence and substance use. *The Journal of Early Adolescence.* 1991;11(1):56-95.

66. Lissa Dutra PD, Georgia Stathopoulou MA, Shawnee L. Basden MA, Teresa M. Leyro BA, Mark B. Powers PD, Michael W. Otto PD. A Meta-Analytic Review of Psychosocial Interventions for Substance Use Disorders. *American Journal of Psychiatry.* 2008;165(2):179-187.

67. Wish ED, Hoffman JA, Nemes S. The validity of self-reports of drug use at treatment admission and at follow-up: Comparisons with urinalysis and hair assays. *NIDA Research Monograph.* 1997;167:200-226.

68. Magura S, Kang S-Y. Validity of self-reported drug use in high risk populations: a meta-analytical review. *Substance Use & Misuse.* 1996;31(9):1131-1153.

69. Alessi SM, Rash, Carla J., Barnett, Nancy P., Petry, Nancy M.,. Most patients in outpatient clinics continue drinking during treatment. Research Society on Alcoholism; 2016; New Orleans, LA.

70. Krumpal I. Determinants of social desirability bias in sensitive surveys: a literature review. *Quality & Quantity.* 2013;47(4):2025-2047.

71. Goldstein RZ, Craig AD, Bechara A, et al. The Neurocircuitry of Impaired Insight in Drug Addiction. *Trends in Cognitive Sciences.* 2009;13(9):372-380.

72. Witkiewitz K, Marlatt GA. Modeling the complexity of post-treatment drinking: It's a rocky road to relapse. *Clinical Psychology Review.* 2007;27(6):724-738.

73. Witkiewitz K, Masyn KE. Drinking trajectories following an initial lapse. *Psychology of Addictive Behaviors.* 2008;22(2):157.

About the Author

A di Jaffe, PhD, is the founder of IGNTD—Igniting Lives Beyond Limits — and a nationally recognized expert on mental health, addiction, and stigma. He lectures in the psychology department at UCLA and was the executive-director and co-founder of one of the most progressive mental health treatment facilities in the country.

Dr. Jaffe's work and research focus on changing the way Americans think about and deal with mental health issues, including the processes of addiction and change. He is passionate about addressing the role of shame in destroying lives and aims to greatly reduce the stigma of mental health in this country. In this context, Dr. Jaffe has used his personal experience with the challenges of addiction, the criminal justice system, and recovery as a powerful tool for inspiration and motivation. His research and views have been published in dozens of journals and publications and he has appeared on numerous television shows and documentaries discussing addiction, therapy, and related social issues. His TEDx talks on shame and the true struggles of transformation have been viewed over six hundred thousand times.

Dr. Jaffe now directs IGNTD and the IGNTD Recovery programs and writes for *Psychology Today* and other publications. His goal is to bring the latest knowledge about addiction to the people who could benefit from it most—those who are suffering because of it—and lead people to more fulfilled lives and relationships than they ever thought possible.

88529529R00071

Made in the USA
San Bernardino, CA
15 September 2018